Beauty for Ashes

Leanna Lacy Roe

Beauty for Ashes
Leanna Lacy Roe
Copyright © 2023

ISBN 9798375198965

Scripture references are taken from the New Living Translation of the Bible unless otherwise noted.

DEDICATION

For our sweet son Jason who fought the fight and kept the
faith and for his precious wife Lana who stood by his side
until she placed him in the arms of Jesus.

TABLE OF CONTENTS

Pages

ACKNOWLEDGEMENTS

I would like to thank my precious husband who endured hours alone as I wrote and rewrote this book. You are my life, my love, my dearest friend.

To my children Matt and Megan, the jewels in my crown, thank you for not being afraid to tell me the truth in love.

To my sister cousins: Ellen, Sally, Martha, and Missy for praying for me.

To my sister-in-law, Ree for crying with me.

To my beautiful Beauty for Ashes team: Kristie, Donna, Beth, Jennie, Robin, Martha, Ann, and Sherri. You have all been such a blessing and encouragement. Without your urging, this book wouldn't be a reality.

To my parents Alfred and Mae Lacy, who are even now worshipping at the throne of God, thank you for teaching me a love for the word and for being Jesus to me.

And finally, to Yvonne, who edited and tweaked and stayed awake at night, you are a friend beyond compare.

And a heartfelt thank you for friends and acquaintances who read what I write and keep asking for more.

FOREWORD

Many of us come to Jesus worn out, emotionally devastated, and having a feeling of hopelessness. Some of us are stuck in the muck and mire of our sin. Others are burdened by pride and self-will. However, on that day when we come mourning to Jesus and ask Him to forgive us and to be our Lord and Master, something awesome happens.

This is not a pity party, rather we mourn that we have left Him out of our plans, our actions, our attitudes, and our choices.

The old mourner's bench had its place. Sinners knelt at an altar and sometimes stayed for hours mourning their sin and repenting. When they got up from that place, it was easy to discern their changed countenance and thereafter to witness their changed life. They now lived in beauty instead of ashes.

By His shed blood, Jesus cleanses us—spirit, soul, and body. When He completes His cleansing work, what's left is ashes! He takes them away, and in their place gives us a glorious glow—His beauty. Our mourning turns into joy. We've been washed squeaky clean. His beauty represents our new life in Him. Now the Light of His Word in us shines out—maybe looking like a "halo" to others who knew us before.

As you read the following pages, you will be encouraged, motivated, and rained upon by fire of the Holy Spirit. Rejoice! He loves to take your ashes and shower you with His beauty.

-C. Yvonne Karl

PREFACE

Dearest Beautiful and Beloved ones,

I have undergone the transforming power of God while sitting in a cold heap of ashes. I have experienced the resurrection power of Jesus as I was raised from despair and I watched my grief and pain transform into something beautiful. I have learned, as I hope you will, there is joy in the journey and life after loss.

My prayer is, as you read these pages, you will see the heart and hand of God, and that hope will abound in your heart.

I promise you, the rain will eventually stop, the sun will shine again, and you will be filled with joy and peace that comes from trusting the One Who loves you more than you can possibly imagine. Live life to the fullest, trusting Jesus all the way!

Leanna

1
How Big Is God?

Our names are engraved on the palms of His hands.
Isaiah 49:16

My first thought as I read this was, "Wow, those are some mighty big hands." And then the tears came. His hands hold me, He knows my name. I am important to Him. What a precious truth!

I tend to underestimate God at times. I remind myself that he isn't just a great big me. He is Infinite, He is Almighty, He is All Powerful, He is my healer, He is my Sustainer, He is my Rock, He is my Fortress, He is my Provider, He is my Father. Of all that God is to me, Father is my absolute favorite title. I can climb up on his lap and be held. He supports me when I'm hurting, He rejoices over me with singing, He comforts me when I'm grieving. He can do things beyond my imagination.

If we could only grasp how much He loves us. I know we question when difficulty, death, and denial come our way. We wonder why He allows it. I don't know, I really don't, and after experiencing many of the aforementioned, I have learned it's not my business to know, it's my business to trust! I can promise you; He works in everything for our good.

Have you hit a rough patch? Do you feel as though your world is falling apart? Are you looking for answers when you don't even know the question? God gets you! He really does. And if it's important to you, it's important to Him. In Hebrews 1:3 we are told that Jesus upholds EVERYTHING by the word of his power. So, if He holds the world up and keeps it spinning on its axis, I think He can handle what you are facing today.

Exactly how big are God's hands? They are big enough.

Prayer

Father,

    What a blessing to know you are big enough! You are enough for whatever I need today, every day, and forever.

    In Jesus' Mighty Name, Amen!

2
Blessings

After a very hectic week, I found myself needing some spiritual R&R. I retired to my office and began to listen to worship songs on my phone. As I listened, the strains of that beautiful song Blessings began to pour forth. What a powerful song! I loved that song! I'm sure many of you have as well.

> What if your blessings come through raindrops?
> What if your healing comes through tears?
> What if a thousand sleepless nights
> Are what it takes to know You're near?
> What if trials of this life are your mercies in disguise?
> (Lyrics by Laura Story)

Beloved, I've had so many blessings in the rainy days of my life. During the darkest, stormiest nights, the light of the love of Jesus has filled me completely. I was loved and comforted by the God who understood exactly how I felt. He'd watched His Son suffer and die, too.

I've been healed through tears. During the times of lying prostrate on the floor and crying out to God, "Why?," I have learned what it means to trust even when I can't begin to understand the ways of the Father.

During those nights as I lay awake wondering "what if," the presence of God was tangible as He held me when no one else but He and I were awake.

I cherish the time spent in my Father's arms learning to trust again. Eventually the sun began to shine, and the flowers began to bloom as beauty arose from the ashes of my grief.

Prayer

Father,

I look back and wonder how I made it through the hours, days, and weeks of suffering. Oh, but then I remember your faithfulness, which is new every morning.

Thank you for always being awake and aware when I need solace. I need You so much.

In Jesus' perfect Name, Amen!

3
You Are Valued

We can all easily find ourselves in an overprotective state of mind, wanting to collect and hold on tightly to everything that brings us comfort and security in the midst of uncertainty.

In Mark 14:3-9, we see the account of a woman who learned how to lay the most precious thing that she owned at the feet of Jesus:

"While He was in Bethany, reclining at the table in the home of Simon the Leper, a woman came with an alabaster jar of very expensive perfume, made of pure nard. She broke the jar and poured the perfume on His head. Some of those present were saying indignantly to one another, 'Why this waste of perfume? It could have been sold for more than a year's wages and the money given to the poor.' And they rebuked her harshly. 'Leave her alone,' said Jesus. 'Why are you bothering her? She has done a beautiful thing to me'."

You see, this lady was not a "churchgoer." She wasn't the type who had everything together. She had a past, and everyone in that room with Jesus knew about it. She was a big-time sinner in their book. And even though she didn't have it all together, she understood something very significant: that she was valued by Jesus. He had forever impacted her life. Jesus wasn't waiting for her to get everything together. He already valued her.

What got the attention of Jesus wasn't her eloquent words, or a life that was refined, but the fact that she gave her absolute all to Him. She took her earthly possessions and laid them at the feet of Jesus. What she was showing Him was true "worth-ship." She was telling Jesus that He was worthy to hold the most important part of her life.

Maybe today, as you are isolated in your own thoughts, you are flooded with accusations about your past, or you are feeling like you don't know how to approach God. I want to encourage you to take the things that you find yourself holding most tightly and lay them at the feet of Jesus. We can take the Alabaster Box of our family, our dreams, careers, fears, and worries, and pour them out at the feet of Jesus.

Prayer

Father,

Only you know what the oil in our personal alabaster boxes has cost us.

Thank you for the miracle of grace you have worked in the lives of those who will come to you for forgiveness.

Thank you for bringing beauty from the ashes of our failures.

In Jesus' redeeming Name,
Amen!

4

Not Our Business

It's hard to see our Enemies flourish. It's mind boggling to see them go on their merry way, prospering and continuing to leave chaos in their wake. It's even harder when you see them "casting their spell" on innocent, unsuspecting victims. You want to scream from the highest mountain, "Watch out, they are going to try and do you in!"

David knew a thing or two about that when he wrote Psalm 55:12-14:

If an enemy were insulting me, I could endure it; if a foe were rising against me, I could hide. But it is you, a man like myself, my companion, my close friend, with whom I once enjoyed sweet fellowship at the house of God, as we walked about among the worshipers.

He was most likely referring to his friend, Ahithophel, the one in whom he confided, with whom he conferred and from whom he sought counsel. And when Absalom, David's son rebelled against David, Ahithophel supported that rebellious young man. How heartbreaking that must have been for David!

Jesus knew what it was like to walk with someone day after day, only to be betrayed by the kiss of evil. Judas! What was he thinking? How could he have betrayed the One who loved him most?

We have all experienced, at least once in our lives, a time when someone we thought was our friend betrayed us. And the worst part is they never ever admitted they were wrong or ever asked for forgiveness. We all know we must forgive them, or God will not forgive us. It's difficult, even as a Christian to say, "You ripped my heart out, you betrayed me, and planned Evil against me, but I forgive you." It's hard, but it's not an option.

It takes prayer and a constant guarding of our hearts so that the root of bitterness doesn't spring up!

I was thinking about a particular incident today. The devil was trying to get me stirred up, when I heard the spirit of God speak ever so softly to my agitated spirit. "You are blessed with good health. Your family is blessed with good health. You are blessed beyond measure with good things, and you have everything you need. What if you could see your enemy pay for what they did, but you were sick or someone you loved was sick? What if you suddenly lost everything that was dear to you? Would all of this matter so much?" The answer was a resounding "NO!"

I began to thank the Lord for his goodness to me and as I did, the desire for vengeance left and peace came to my heart. When Peter asked what would happen to John, Jesus replied, "What is that to you; follow me." Jesus basically said, "That's not your business. Your business is to follow me." And I heard those same words. "What is that to you, Leanna, just walk in your calling. What others do isn't any of your business. Your business is to walk in obedience to me." In other words, let it go."

I am always amazed and astounded at the wonderful love and grace of God. He just keeps working on us even when we are tempted to go off the deep end about something that is His concern, not ours. How patiently he teaches us that his ways are the best ways.

And so, once again, I turn my eyes on the One who is able. The One who is worthy! The One who is holy. The One who will guide us by the skillfulness of His hands until we finally reach our heavenly home. As we think on that, it makes all the rest seem so insignificant.

How about you? Are you obsessed with revenge? Are you concerned because the one who nearly destroyed you, who betrayed your trust, seems to be enjoying life without a care in the world? Beloved, it's not your business. It's God's!

Right now, ask God to forgive you for allowing your mind to be assailed by things over which you have no control. Ask him to help you forgive the one who left you feeling less than you are. And move on! It may take some time. I assure you it will take prayer; it will take effort. But in the end, you will have victory. Stop allowing the devil to rob you of your joy. Keep on keeping on! You cannot even begin to imagine what God has in store for you.

Prayer

Father,

Please help me as I seek to forgive the one(s) who have hurt me so deeply. I can't do it on my own. Make me willing and help me to stop allowing the enemy to keep me focused on what was done to me. I want to be free!

In Jesus' Name,
Amen!

Notes

5
Led by the Spirit

Then Jesus, full of the Holy Spirit,
returned from the Jordan River.
He was led by the Spirit in the wilderness,
where He was tempted by the devil for forty days.
Jesus ate nothing all that time and became very hungry.
Luke 4:1-2

Did you catch that? Jesus was LED into the wilderness. The Holy Spirit LED him into the wilderness where He was tempted by the devil. I confess, I never caught that in all the times I've read that passage. This time it grabbed my attention. We know the Holy Spirit is our guide, but to lead us to a place where we will face hardship and trial? Well, I just never thought of it that way. And yet He led the very Son of God to a wilderness experience.

Hebrews 5:8 tells us that Jesus learned obedience through the things He suffered. Could it be that Jesus, fully God, fully man, learned something from that desolate, deserted, depressing place where he was LED?

The wilderness is uninhabited by humans, there are no paths. Jesus was alone and He was hungry and at His weakest point, the devil jumped on the opportunity. He tempted Jesus to make bread out of stones. We know perfectly well, Jesus could have, but He said, "Man doesn't live by bread alone." In other words, "Yes, I'm hungry, but I'm depending on my Father. He will give me what I need!"

Again, the devil struck. This time he offered Jesus all the kingdoms of the world if Jesus would only bow down to Him. I find it interesting that the devil offered what wasn't his to offer, to the One who created and owned it all! Satan is like that. He

11

makes promises he can't keep, and he offers that which is not his to offer. Jesus threw the WORD at him, "You must worship the Lord your God and serve only him."

The devil tried once again by leading Jesus to the pinnacle of the temple in Jerusalem. He said, "If you really are WHO you say you are, then jump, because the scriptures say, 'He will order His angels to protect and guard you. They will hold you up in their hands, so you won't even hurt your foot on a stone'." Isn't that ludicrous? The very idea that the devil would quote scripture to the One who inspired it. Remember this: the WORD of God has no power in the hands of the devil, and he knows it. Seriously, you have to shake your head. And Jesus replied, "Don't tempt the Lord Your God!" My interpretation of that is. "I AM GOD! Don't mess with me!" Isn't it a hoot to watch how Jesus handles the evil one? And the devil left Him, but get this, the Bible says, "he [the devil] left Him until the next opportunity presented itself. The devil fought Jesus until Jesus' last breath.

I said all that to say this. Today, you may find yourself in a hard place. Sometimes we find ourselves in hard places because of decisions we have made, and I believe the Spirit sometimes leads us to situations to teach us lessons we couldn't learn otherwise. And please know this, the devil loves to kick you when you're down. He will find you at your weakest point, just like he did Jesus, but be assured today
- You have the Father's arms to carry you.
- You have the blood of Jesus to cover you.
- You have the Holy Spirit to comfort and sustain you.

Spend time in prayer and in the Word today in preparation for the next opportunity the devil seizes to try to take you down. Be held by the power of God!

Prayer

Father,

Help me to recognize the voice of the enemy and to submit myself to you, resist the devil and he will start running. There is power in Your Name and power in Your word.

Thank you for the wonder working power of the blood You shed for me.

In Your sweet Name I pray,
Amen!

Notes

6
Put Yourself out There!

To have a friend, you have to be a friend. To have friends you have to be friendly. I remember once I came home from church and said to my Mama, "Sister So and So didn't speak to me." "Hmmm," replied my Mama, "did you speak to her?" Well, my goodness, that never occurred to me. I'm so thankful I had a Mama who kept it real. So, I'm going to be real with you today. I am an introvert who became an extrovert because I had to.

My Mama used to make me sing at church and I hated it. I would be sick for a week just worrying about getting up in front of people! And at school, Lord, have mercy, they were always after me to sing for this or that. In fact, I made my debut in the fifth-grade singing, "O Holy Night." I wore a pink dress and ruffled socks, and I thought I was going to have a breakdown before the whole ordeal was behind me. People still say, "Leanna, I remember when you sang "Oh Holy Night" for the Christmas program at school." And I reply, "Oh yes, so do I." It was a living nightmare.

I grew up and married a minister. Let me tell you, as a pastor's wife I learned to put myself out there. I had nightmares of reaching out to shake hands with someone and saying, "Hi, I'm Leanna Roe!" only to hear them say, "So what?" But I did it anyway and desensitized myself to being shy and withdrawn. And I'm so glad I did. There are folks we see that need a hug, a handshake and word of appreciation or encouragement. Isn't that what the body of Christ is all about?

Today, I want you to try something. Go out of your way to speak to someone. The next time you are at church, find someone who doesn't really get a lot of attention, shake their hand, make them feel special, offer a word of encouragement

15

to them. And if you are shy and one of those people who doesn't like to leave your little corner of contentment, stand up, take a deep breath, and go to the person nearest you, stick out your hand, tell them you're glad to see them. You may never know what that small gesture will mean to someone who is having a bad day, or who is walking through a storm.

Prayer

Father,

Help me to stop being concerned about what others think of me and help me to think of others.

Give me the courage I need to help someone know how special and loved they are, just like you do me every day of my life.

In Jesus' strong Name, Amen!

7
God is Working

Moses spoke to the people:
"Don't be afraid. Stand firm and watch GOD do His work of
salvation for you today. Take a good look at the Egyptians
today for you're never going to see them again.
GOD will fight the battle for you.
And you? You keep your mouths shut!"
Exodus 14:13-14

So, you think you've waited on God long enough. You think you should have had a WORD from God. You should have had an answer by now. You feel so out of the loop. Why isn't God letting you know what the next step is? The situation is getting precarious, you don't have a clue how things will play out, but you can't just sit on your hands and wait, you have to take matters into your own hands and make something happen before disaster strikes.

Oh, you are in dangerous territory! Just because you aren't hearing from God doesn't mean He isn't working. He IS working. He is putting things in place so that you will have a beautiful afterward. He has a plan that will amaze and astound you. But if you try to take charge, you are going to get in the way of the perfect plan God has for you and you are going to get so far out of His will that it may take years for you to get back where you need to be.

In the not so long ago, I remember wanting to get out of certain set of circumstances. God wasn't doing anything that I could see, so I decided to take matters in my own hands. I'm horrified as I look back at the mess I made. It took years, about thirteen in fact, to get back to the will of God for my life. And while the joy of the Lord was my strength as I struggled to come

17

to terms with what my doing had caused, there were times when I was miserable.

The Israelites were in dire straits, weren't they? Pharaoh's army behind them and the Red Sea before them. Their answer to the problem was to just surrender and go back to being slaves in Egypt. Oh, but God had some big plans the likes of which those fraidy cat Israelites had never seen. Like us, they wanted instant gratification, and they were so afraid they just wanted out of the place they were in. They were willing to go back to slavery rather than throw all they had on to the shoulders of the only One who could solve their problem.

Moses told them to just keep their mouths shut and watch what God would do. Oh, my goodness, I know there are times when God should say that to us. And He does but He is a little kinder with His words. "Be still, trust me, I've got this." He is so good. He loves us so much and sometimes we all forget that.

God told Moses, "Tell the people to keep on going, and while you're at it, raise your rod over the sea." Then the angel of the Lord who had been leading this march, and the pillar of cloud also moved behind them. God was putting his plan in place.

Moses raised the rod and get this; the sea didn't part right then. Oh, I love this; all night long God caused a strong east wind to blow. And in the morning, the people began to cross over ON. DRY. GROUND.

When the Egyptian armies came after them, those soldiers got stuck in the mud and looking down from the Pillar of Fire, God caused them to panic. Well, we all know the end of the story. The water came crashing down on top of the Egyptians, their horses, and chariots. But on the other side of the Red Sea, the Israelites were safe and sound. Look what they would have missed if they had not waited on God.

When we step on the Father's toes while we are trying to solve our problems, we often find ourselves in a place of misery and regret. Can you imagine what kind of misery the Israelites faced if they had had their way? Back to slavery, a return to back breaking, no appreciation, the king couldn't care less about them, work. And now they stood on the beach at the Red Sea and saw God annihilate their enemies. They were free! All of us at one time or another have said, "If I had only waited on God, I wouldn't be in this fix." The moral of the story is this: if you think you're in a mess now, just try to be God.

Beloved, you haven't seen a mess until you think you're smarter and more capable than God.

God wants to do the unimaginable, the indescribable, the incredible for us and He will if we wait. And while we wait, we worship and we remind ourselves that even though we can't see it this side of the veil, He is working to get us across our Red Sea.

Sit tight! Keep praying! Trust completely in His divine ability and love! God's way out may not be the easy way out, but it's the best way!

Prayer

Father,

Waiting is so hard. We look for a signal to move and there's nothing. We keep hearing you say, "stay still." Help us to trust you. You have never failed us, and you never will. We know waiting will bring wonderful, amazing results when we keep our mouths shut, our spirits quiet, and our hearts fully engaged with yours. We are waiting and watching.
In Jesus, strong Name, Amen!

Notes

8
Don't Worry. Be Happy!

Don't worry about anything; instead, pray about
everything. Tell God what you need
and thank him for all He has done.
Then you will experience God's peace, which exceeds
anything we can understand. His peace will guard your
hearts and minds as you live in Christ Jesus.
Philippians 4:6-7

There you have it, the recipe for peace in a world gone crazy. Don't worry about anything, pray about everything, tell God what you need, thank Him for all He has done.

Ah, then, you will experience God's peace and that peace is something the world can't give, and the world can't take away. No problem, circumstance, difficulty, illness, relationship issue, can take away our joy, if we stop worrying, start praying, telling God about what is bothering us, (before we tell anyone else), and then thank Him for what He has done what He is doing now and thank Him for what He is going to do in response to your prayer. I dare you to try this. It is a promise from God. And if He said He would, then He will!

Stop listening to the devil. He is a liar, and he loves to torment you. Don't give him satisfaction. Live in peace, joy, and victory today. This is the will of God for us all!

PRAYER

Father, So many times I run to the phone instead of the throne. I tell my best friend, who may be sympathetic, but who really can't give me what I need. Forgive me for those times. Help me to remember that You are my source, and You will provide what I need. In Jesus' Name, Amen!

Notes

9
Don't Let Fear Win

October is Breast Cancer Awareness month. I am aware. I am very aware! Am I ever! When I was fifteen, my maternal grandmother passed away from breast cancer. It had a profound impact on my life. When it's time for a mammogram, I go into panic mode. I have to constantly pray that God will give me peace and help me not to worry.

I experienced those moments of panic again this year as I prepared for my visit to the Imaging Center. Somewhere on the way, God lifted the fear, and I did what I needed to do. Oh, but wait! I still needed to get the results. So many what ifs began to roil through my mind. It suddenly occurred to me that the negativity and fear were not from my Father, who loves me so much. They were straight from the pit of hell. Fear is not of God!

Now, I'm ashamed of myself because I've been saved a very long time, been through a good many things, and God has proved faithful every time! I'm pleased to say my results were good. But what if they hadn't been? Would that change who God is? Would that mean He isn't faithful? Would that mean He isn't good? NO, and no again, absolutely not, no way!

No matter what our circumstances, good or bad, no matter the outcome, God is good and faithful and great! The fact is, when we face trials of any kind, He is there supporting us with His strong right arm, holding us in the palm of His hand and filling us with grace to face the unexpected happenings we call life.

The New Testament writer James knew a thing or two about trials. He says: *Consider it a sheer gift, friends, when tests and challenges come at you from all sides. You know that under pressure, your faith-life is forced into the open and shows its true colors. So don't try to get out of anything prematurely. Let it do its work, so you become mature and well-developed, not deficient in any way* (James 1:1-4 MSG).

Jesus knew something about trials, too, and He was victorious in every one of them. Why? Because He depended on His Father to provide what was needed in every situation. Even though Jesus was God's Son, He learned obedience from the things He suffered (Hebrews 5:8). Now that is something to hold on to. If Jesus, the very Son of God, learned obedience through suffering then who do we think we are? Our very reason for existence is to be conformed to the image of Jesus. So, if He suffered, well, hold on to your hat, so will we. It's a given. Being a Child of God doesn't exempt us from suffering. Surprise! Surprise!

If you have never been through what I call "the long dark night of the soul," you will one day! And I promise you (I know this from experience), Jesus will be with you. The fellowship you have during your season of suffering will be sweeter than you can ever imagine. The lessons you learn as you become still in His presence will never be forgotten. And you will emerge from the darkness with a greater understanding of His love for you.

Prayer

Father,

Help me to trust you even when the circumstances of my life seem insurmountable. Help me to remember Who You are. Help me to cling to You. Help me to experience the joy of the journey with you. I know you will never leave me. I know your grace will sustain me. And I know that in your good time, I will come forth as gold, understanding more than ever Your goodness.

In Jesus strong name, Amen!

10
We're Not Home Yet

My Father's house has many rooms;
if that were not so I would have told you.
I am going to prepare a place for you.
John 14:2

I listen to Christmas Carols all year long, especially on dark rainy days. Why not? I tell myself that I want to make sure I'm mentally and emotionally prepared. "I'll be Home for Christmas" is one of my favorite secular Christmas songs, and yet it makes my heart hurt, because I know our son will not be home for Christmas this year or any other year. His smile will never light up our world. His laughter will never ring again through the rooms of our home.

A burst of grief caught me unaware. And then my Father, who understands my grief and pain spoke to my spirit. "Jason IS home, you are the one who isn't!" The reality of that truth rocked me and then thrilled me to my socks. This place I call home, isn't really. It's my stopping-off place. My house is no more than a bed and breakfast, a place to stay until I finally reach the destination where I was created to live forever.

Can you comprehend it? We aren't home yet! This place, where we spend our days, isn't the destination; it's part of the journey. It's the place that prepares us for our heavenly home. The Bible is clear that Jesus has prepared a place for us. And it will be perfect. It will have everything we need. It will be beautiful beyond anything we can even begin to fathom. Jesus will be there! And all the questions we ever had while we have been travelling will be answered, if we even care.

Our loved ones are waiting for us to come home! They are living extraordinary lives in an inconceivable place.

They aren't worried about anything. They aren't in pain. They are experiencing eternal joy in the presence of the King. And someday, if we know Jesus, we will all be HOME FOR CHRISTMAS.

Prayer

Father,

When the grief bursts unexpectedly into our day, when burdens get beyond heavy, when our world is spiraling out of control, help us to remember, this is only temporary.

Help us to trust you, to praise you, and to live life to the fullest until we are finally at Home with you and those we love.

In Jesus' comforting Name, Amen!

11
Failure Is Not Final with the Father

If we confess our sins, He is faithful and just forgives our sins and to cleanse us from all unrighteousness.
1 John 1:9

You made a bad choice. The cost was higher than you ever thought it would be. You are paying for it every day. Guilt and shame are almost more than you can bear. You want to sit in the mudhole of your life, shut yourself behind a locked door and hide from everything and everyone.

Come on now. You aren't the first person who ever did something you regret. I would say we all have done things we deeply regret. I know I've done some things I would give almost anything to go back for a do over. Unfortunately, that isn't the way things work.

We have one chance at this thing we call life, and we can't change the past. That's why I'm so thankful for the grace that is greater than all of yours and my sins. That grace says that while we don't deserve to be forgiven, and while we really should have our offense thrown in our face daily, forgiveness and forgetfulness are offered freely to us by the Lord Jesus.

Tears fall as I try to fathom the depth of that wonderful truth. Jesus will not only forgive me, if I ask, but He chooses to forget I ever did it. I'm shaking my head at the thought; my heart is full of wonder that He loves me that much. It's true. That's why he died: so that we might have our sins forgiven. That's why John wrote, "If we confess our sins, He is faithful and just to forgive us of our sins, and to cleanse us from all unrighteousness." There you have it. Now get up and get out of the mud, brush yourself off, take the first step, hold your head up! You are forgiven and free!!

27

Prayer

Father,

I beat myself up, and the devil joins in, with regrets I can do nothing about. Help me to remember my sins have been cast in the depths of the sea never to be remembered against me again. Help me to rise up in power and victory because I belong to you.

In the Name of the One who died that I might live. Amen!

12
Believe God

Without faith it is impossible to please God....
Hebrews 11:6

Many times, when faced with discouragement, the temptation is to give into it. When words are spoken that cut to our hearts, we mull them over in our hearts and before we realize it, we have allowed the enemy to convince us we are of no worth, that we are not loved, that we are unwanted and nonessential.

The enemy roams about trying to find ways to bring us down, not only that, but he literally wants to devour us. He wants to make us ineffective. He wants to cause us to look at the mountain instead of fixing our gaze on the One who is able to remove the mountain. As I began my morning reading in Hebrews 11, the very first verse contained a truth that we all need to grab a hold of and believe with all our hearts.

What is faith? It is the confident assurance that something we want is going to happen. It is the certainty that what we hope for is waiting for us, even though we cannot see it up ahead.

Wow! An arrow of conviction struck my heart. It's all about trusting when we can't see. It's all about not just believing IN God but BELIEVING GOD! It's all about knowing He loves us too much to fail us.... EVER! It's all about giving up control and keeping our hands off. It's about cuddling up close to the Father in prayer, pouring out our needs and praising Him for the answer.

Shame on us for being negative when we are in need! Lord, help us to look at our problems through the lens of your power and ability, not through our puny resources. The God of the Universe is on our side! He has never failed to provide, and He never will.

Can you imagine how it breaks the heart of God to hear us speak words of negativity? Can you even begin to fathom how disappointed He is when we forget WHO we are in Him? The Bible tells us we are the apple of His eye, our names are engraved on the palms of His hands, He knows how many hairs we have on our heads, His eyes are always on us, and His heart is open to us.

He wants us to march forward with confidence. As we continue to walk in obedience to Him, the way opens before us and what we need will be supplied! Wait for it and BELIEVE GOD!!!!!

Prayer

Father,
I do believe you! And I know you are able!
Thank you for loving me and forgive me for doubting you!
In Jesus' Gracious Name,
Amen!

13
Just Ask!

You do not have because you do not ask!
James 4:2

Recently, I was in a meeting where a need was being discussed. Answers were needed and the waiting dragged on. It suddenly occurred to me that I had not once prayed for God to intervene. I wondered why because I'm a great proponent of "pray about absolutely everything." My motto is this: "If it's important to you, it's important to God." And I don't just mean the major things, I mean anything and everything that causes us frustration.

God wants us to come to Him with everything from lost car keys to damaged relationships, to unsaved people we love. His love is boundless, His mercy is endless, His power is unrivaled, and He wants to be involved in our lives.

I think we shut God out of the things we deem less important. We don't want to bother Him with what we believe He sees as trivial. The truth is, there is nothing in our lives that God sees as unimportant. We are the apple of His eye; He has gone to great lengths to show His love and concern for us. He sees everything that is going on with us and He is waiting for us to ask for whatever it is we need.

After that meeting, I made it a point to pray every day for a resolution to the issue at hand. And I began to encourage others to pray and believe with me. I can't wait to see how God answers!

Could it be that we have needs that remain unmet, because we haven't been bold enough to ask? Your Father is waiting for you to climb up on His lap and share those very things with Him. I promise you He will not turn you away and while you are speaking, He will answer you! That's the kind of Father He is.

Today, I dare you to take that question that needs an answer to the ONE who is THE ANSWER. No matter how small you think the need is, it's a big deal to our great big God! Ask Him!

Prayer

Father,

Forgive me for not asking for your help in matters I feel are silly or inconsequential.

Help me to remember that every aspect of my life is important to you.

Forgive me for excluding you from even the smallest issue and help me to begin today to pray about everything.

In Jesus Mighty Name, Amen!

14
Making it Through the Storm

... We also glory in our sufferings because we know that suffering produces perseverance; perseverance, character; and character produces hope.
Romans 5:3-4

I was looking back through one of my prayer journals. That particular year, I had lost my sweet Mama and the grief was almost unbearable. Coupled with that was the feeling I could have done more to comfort her. The "what ifs" swirled through my mind with gale force. I was almost completely undone.

Talk about a rainy day, this was a rainy year. Day after day, I begged God to give me relief and daily I seemed to feel worse. It was as though the foundation of my life had crumbled and I was left hanging, suspended in space, and at any moment, I would freefall! It was the darkest, most miserable time of my life.

And yet, as I look back at the entries in my journal, I see that gradually I began to heal. I see the gracious greatness of God in all of it. He never left my side during all of my moaning and crying and suffering. His Word was the medicine I took daily to sooth my tortured soul. And one day, the sun peeped through the clouds. The rain had stopped. The storm was over. I was battered but not beaten. I was weary but I was wiser. I had been a victim, but I had come through victorious. Oh, the overwhelming, matchless, grace of Jesus. I look back with praise and thanksgiving that He allowed me to experience those moments of profound pain and anguish.

The Bible tells us when we suffer, we are partners in the suffering of Jesus and in the blessed afterward, His glory will be revealed in us. Although Jesus was one hundred percent God, He was also one hundred percent human (figure that one out if you can!). He felt sorrow, He knew what it was to lose people He loved. Oh, and He loves us so much. His love is the one thing in this life of which we can be absolutely, positively sure.

Are you in a rainy season? Hang in there. Let the love and grace of God be your umbrella. Allow the comfort of the Holy Spirit to salve the wounds in your heart. One day you will look back and realize you were never alone. One day you will see the silver lining behind the clouds. One day you will emerge from the rain with a heart more devoted to Jesus than ever before. One day the joy bells will once again ring in your heart. You made it through the storm!

Prayer

Father,

This trial is so hard. I wake up every morning hoping the pain will be gone, but there it is, in my face again.

I need You to help me through this long, lonely downpour. No one understands, but I know You do.

Please give me the strength I need to get to the end of this trial in one piece.

In Jesus Mighty Name, Amen!

15
Living Life to the Fullest

The thief comes not but to steal, kill, and destroy.
I have come so that they may have life and have it more
abundantly.
John 10:10

I want to speak life to you today. Jesus wants you to have abundant, everlasting, peace like a river, joy like a fountain life! It is not His will for you to allow yourself to be defined by past mistakes. He wants you to live in the here and now. Forget about the things that are behind you, nothing can change what has already been! Ah, but Jesus offers a future full of hope!

There have been events in my life that I have buried. The devil loves to dig them up and throw the dirt in my face. I am learning to rebuke and resist him, because it is not God's plan for us to torture ourselves with a "coulda, shoulda, woulda." When we gave ourselves to Jesus, He cast our sins in the deepest sea and the Bible says that He will never go fishing for them. What a promise! What a Father!

Today, whatever is keeping you from having perfect peace and living a rich life, full of the grace of God, lay it down and leave it. We don't have to take what the devil hands out. He is a defeated foe. He knows it, but do you? If you know it, then remind him of it. (He hates it when we do that!)

You do not have to live in bondage. Jesus came to set you free. And if Jesus has made you free, you are free without a doubt. Period! The end! No ifs, ands, or buts! You are His! Rise up in the power of Christ and live life to the fullest, in abundance and all sufficient grace.

Prayer

Father,

Often the devil brings to my mind the poor choices I have made. It makes me feel so worthless.

When these moments come, help me to rely on the power of your gracious faithfulness.

The past is gone.

You don't remember it, so why should I?

Help me not to allow the enemy to pull me into a debate about what has been.

Help me to rise up and remind him of exactly who You are and who I am in You!

Help me to send him on His way.

Thank you, Lord, for loving me. I am depending on You!

In Jesus Strong Name, Amen!

16
Divine Detours

Show me Your ways, O Lord; teach me Your paths.
Psalm 25:4

For nearly ninety-plus days our roads have undergone repaving and repair. Every day it seemed the traffic pattern was changed. Every morning there were traffic jams and fender benders. It seemed we were always trying to find an easier way to get to the office.

One day as I drove to the city, I realized the road had been cleared and the exits were open. And, oh my, they looked good! Instead of it taking me twenty-five minutes to get to my office it took eleven. I have to tell you, I was one thankful gal.

It reminds me of some of the times of my life. Times when nothing was going the way I thought it should! When I wanted to plow straight on through, I had to take detours that were difficult to navigate. Plans that I had made were circumvented by some unseen hand. Time dragged on as I waited for the way to clear, and I would once again be on my merry way.

At some point, however, I stopped struggling, I stopped asking, "why?" and I accepted the diversion. When I did, somehow, the way seemed easier. And then one day, the road became straight, the visibility was crystal clear, and I was able to continue on with joy.

I had made it through the time of waiting and wondering. I had successfully navigated the bypass of my dreams and schemes. I was thankful, because God knows the way that I take and when I'm headed in the wrong direction, He devises a divine detour.

When we trust our Father completely with our lives, we should never fight the deviation of our plans. The Bible tells us that God's plans are higher than our plans. That's God's way of saying, "I'm smarter than you are, stop trying to be me!" He has a design for us that is so much better than the puny plans we try to perpetrate. Slow down! Enjoy the journey!

Prayer

Father,

It seems I'm always in a hurry. I want instant gratification. It's hard to go into the unknown when I have my journey mapped out to my satisfaction.

Help me to follow you even when you lead me into the unfamiliar and less traveled path.

I know you know best.

Help me to find the joy you have prepared for me as I yield totally to your direction.

In Jesus Strong Name, Amen!

17
Jesus Knows. Jesus Cares!

When Jesus saw her weeping,
and the Jews who had come along with her also weeping,
He was deeply moved in spirit and troubled.
John 11:38

I don't know about you, but it touches something deep inside me to know Jesus was deeply moved in His spirit at the news that Lazarus had died. How many of us wonder where He is when we have lost the dearest thing in life to us? Well, I think this scripture answers that question. He is right there, tears streaming, as He beholds our heartbreak.

Hebrews 4:15 says: *For we do not have a high priest who is unable to empathize with our weaknesses ....*

Jesus knows what it's like to suffer, to lose someone He loved, to be deserted, to be talked about. He knows what it feels like for someone to spit in His face, to mock Him, to beat Him! He knows what it is to be totally forsaken. As He hung on the cross, the sin He carried was so great that God could not look on it. He was alone. He never wants us to experience the terror of that kind of total isolation and so He promised: *I will never leave you Or forsake you (*Hebrews 13: 5).

Never, not ever, not under any circumstance, will Jesus leave you. He is a present Savior. He is in the here and now! He is in the midst of your storm. He is in the heat of your battle; He is in the middle of your heartache.

Take a deep breath. Sense His presence. Be comforted! Be held! He is there!

Prayer

Lord Jesus,
My heart hurts.
When no one understands what I'm going through, it's comforting to know that you understand and care.
Thank You that you will never leave me.
Thank You for your sweet presence, Your arms that hold me and your grace that keeps me.
In Jesus mighty Name, Amen!

18
You Can Make It!

In His kindness God called you to share in
His eternal glory
by means of Christ Jesus.
So, after you have suffered a little while,
He will restore, support, and strengthen you,
and He will place you on a firm foundation.
I Peter 5:10

The sun is shining today. The view outside my office is of some stubborn, dead, brown leaves hanging on to dull gray tree limbs. But as I continue scrutinizing the landscape, I see in the distance a tiny red birdhouse, boldly taking its stand amidst the various shades of brown and gray. It stands like a beacon. It provides shelter for the brave little birds who took a chance and remained here in our fickle climes.

For me it's even more. It inspires me and enables me to remember that winter doesn't last forever, and that spring will make its appearance when we least expect it. Soon we will see lovely little blue birds fluttering near the red birdhouse. Life is like that. The cold gray winter of depression, grief, and pain can make us feel as though things will never change. We are imprisoned and isolated, but if we look closely, we will see signs of hope and relief off in the distance.

Gradually, the bleak winter fades into the colors of spring, and the sun shines again. Looking back, we wonder how we were able to survive, but here we are. We made it through winter season of our lives with a will to go on. As we are exposed to the sunshine, we begin to blossom once again. We thought our world had dissolved into ashes, but we find ourselves smiling again, reaching out once more, and intentionally living life to the fullest.

Prayer

Father,
I know that life can be good.
I know you want me to have peace.
You said, "Let not your heart be troubled."
When my heart, mind, spirit, and soul are troubled,
    help me to turn to you for peace the world knows
    nothing about and accept it.
Thank you for being ever so patient with me.
In Jesus' strong Name.
Amen!

19
He Is There

And be sure of this:
I am with you always,
even to the end of the age.
Matthew 28:20

As I lay in my bed of affliction, inebriated from the ingestion of enough cough syrup to knock an elephant off its feet, (I would be hard pressed to walk a straight line; that stuff is powerful) I ruminate on the precious memories of this holiday season. However, the mess around me has me concerned.

My Christmas tree still stands, naked now, as a testimony to the state of the residents in this household. (Just so you know, only the tree is naked.) To my credit, I managed to take the decorations down, but have yet to get the tree put away. I exerted every ounce of energy on that usually minor task. And so, I decided the tree will have to quiver in its state of undress until I get another spurt of energy.

The living room looks like an explosion of a Christmas shop. This year I decided I would be intentionally organized in putting my Christmas decorations away. Oh, I was organized. I know exactly which pile holds what. I can only be thankful I don't have to worry about anyone stopping by, because everyone is afraid of me. And I don't blame them. I look terrible, I sound terrible, I feel terrible. So, I guess that makes me terrible.

Being shut in for two or three days is okay if you have planned a retreat of sorts, but when you get knocked down with whatever this nastifcation (I make up words to fit the occasion and nasty can't begin to describe whatever it is that ails me) is, you can't enjoy it. It's cough, sneeze, blow, repeat! And do you know how much energy all of that takes?

It was all I could to do to take a shower and fix something to eat. I mean you can't even enjoy food when everything tastes like it just came fresh from Meade Papermill. Honestly, I'm trying to find an upside here and I'm blank!

And in addition, why couldn't it snow whilst I couldn't get out? I've had enough of being shut up like a prisoner in solitary confinement to last me for a while. And I'm sure just when I get to feeling better and am out and about doing what I love to do, it will snow knee deep and I will have to stay in AGAIN!

To all those who have suffered the same fate as I have, my utmost sympathy! This has not been fun!

But seriously, sometimes during the "knock-down" times, God is able to do a work in us that He couldn't have if we had been frenetically going about our daily lives. I confess, during this time, I have not felt much like praying, and yet, my Father was just a whisper away. So many times, during the past week, I have breathed His Name and I knew He was near. You see, He isn't afraid of catching what we have. He is immune to sickness, but He isn't immune to our misery. And He knows sometimes we just need to rest in Him and stop trying so hard. I'm glad I belong to Him.

Wherever you are today, sick, disheartened, hurting, disappointed, hopeless, He is there. And He will always be! Just reach out and touch Him!

Prayer

Father: During the days we are incapacitated by illness, sometimes, we don't feel well enough to pray. The good news is, we can breathe your Name and know you've been there with us in the mess. You are good, even when things are not. I love being your child. Thank you. In Jesus' Name. Amen!

20
Do Your Best and God Will Do the Rest

Trust in the LORD with all your heart;
do not depend on your own understanding.
Seek his will in all you do,
and he will show you which path to take.
Psalm 3:5-6

Ruth's husband had died. Her mother-in-law, Naomi, had lost both her husband and her two sons. Naomi, not wanting to live away from her family in Bethlehem, decided to go back home. Ruth refused to remain behind, and she moved right along with her beloved mother-in-law.

Ruth didn't let any grass grow under her feet once they got settled. One day she said, "I'm going to work." I'm going out to find a field where I can find some harvesters who will be kind to me and let me gather what they leave behind. She eventually ended up in a field owned by Boaz who, get this, was related to Ruth's deceased father-in-law. Me thinks I see the hand of God working on Ruth and Naomi's behalf.

Boaz wonders about this beautiful young woman gleaning in his fields. And the harvesters give Ruth a glowing recommendation. "She is that Moabite gal who came with Naomi from Moab. She asked permission to gather after your harvesters and she hasn't even stopped for a break, and she's been here since the crack of dawn." (Leanna version)

Boaz is fascinated, and he takes Ruth under his wing so to speak. He tells her she will be safe in his fields. He lets her know that the young men won't bother her (I'm thinking he staked his claim on Ruth then and there), and when she needs a drink, she is to go right ahead and drink from the buckets his servants have filled. (Oh, yes, he is interested!)

Boaz goes on say that he is super impressed with her treatment of Naomi and assures her God will reward her for being so faithful.

Well, one thing leads to another, and Ruth and Boas marry. Are you surprised? (For the full story, Read the book of Ruth.) She gives birth to Obed, and they live happily ever after.

The thing that is so notable about Ruth is that she didn't sit down and let depression and fear overtake her. She did something. She was determined to find a way to feed herself and Naomi and when she persevered, God provided exactly what she needed and even more!

God has promised to supply our needs, but He expects us to do our part. If we do what we CAN do, God will do what we CANNOT!

Our daughter often says, "Do your best until you can do better!" Isn't that what Ruth did? Obviously, she didn't have many marketable skills, but she found something to do, she did her best, and her hard work caught the attention of the man who was the answer to her prayers.

You may, at this very moment, find yourself in a place where you really aren't sure which way to turn. Seek the face of God. He will direct you and enable you to do whatever it is you need to do. And when you do your best, He will do the rest.

Oh, did I mention that Boaz, Obed, and Ruth are all in the lineage of Jesus, right along with Rahab (the prostitute) who, incidentally, was Boaz' mother. Wow, God!

Ruth had every reason to just sit in the cold ashes of her life, but she refused to allow her sorrow and loss to keep her there. She got up and got moving and the next thing she knew, the ashes had been replaced with beauty!

Prayer

Father,
Today, I need help. I need directions.
I need your hand to help me up.
Help me to be willing, like Ruth, to do whatever it takes.
I know if I do what I can do, you will do what I can't.
Thank you in advance. In Jesus' Name, Amen!

Notes

21
She Was What?

It was by faith that Rahab the prostitute
was not destroyed with the people
in her city who refused to obey God.
For she had given a friendly welcome to the spies.
Hebrews 11:31

Rahab was a popular gal. She had people coming and going from her home day and night. Of course, her visitors were mostly men, because you see, Rahab made her living by selling her favors to them. She was a prostitute!

I'm sure Rahab longed for deliverance and wanted a better life for herself. She was in a position in which many women find themselves. She had a family, mother, father, brothers, sisters. I wonder if she was their sole support. And, well, she may not have had many skills except (ahem) for that one. And like others who have found themselves in the same circumstances, I believe she wanted a new life. She wanted to be able to look in the mirror in the morning and like what she saw. She wanted to feel good about herself.

The opportunity of a lifetime presented itself in the form of two spies who took refuge in her house. She not only gave them shelter, but she protected them from the king and his men. Why? Because, as she so succinctly said, "I know all God has done, how He dried up the Red Sea and you passed over on dry ground. I know God is God in heaven and on earth" (Joshua 2:9-11). She made a confession of faith. And she didn't know it then, but, oh my, her life was about to make a 180-degree turn. She thought she was bargaining for her life and that of her family, but she got way more than she bargained for.

Oh, I love this story. So, girls, here's what happened. Rahab and her family joined the caravan of the Israelites. On down the road, (literally) Rahab met a man named Salmon and they had a son named Boaz who went on to marry Ruth. You know, the gal a book of the Bible was named after? That's not all. Jesus was a descendent of Boaz who was related to King David. Yep, she was in the lineage of the Holy Savior of the world.

I love when God just has a hay-day in our lives. He does that when we are at the end of ourselves and turn to Him. He did marvelous things for Rahab, and she is even in the Hall of Faith in the Book of Hebrews (check it out, Hebrews 11). And He wants to do that for each of us. He is waiting patiently for us to come and lay the ashes of our lives at His feet. And, when we do, He will restore us, clean us up, and give us a reason to live. He will bring beauty from our ashes!!

Prayer

Father,

I'm thankful it doesn't matter what I've done, or where I came from, or who "my people" are.

I've been adopted into the Family of God. And it feels so good to know you love me in spite of who I used to be.

I'm yours!
Thank you!
In Jesus' Name, Amen!

22
God's Will or Mine

Paul and his companions
traveled throughout the region of Phrygia and Galatia,
having been kept by the Holy Spirit
from preaching the word in the provinces of Asia.
When they came to the border of Mysia,
they tried to enter Bithynia,
but the Spirit of Jesus would not allow them to.
Acts 16:6-7

Paul and his ministry team were forbidden by the Spirit to go into Asia. They had planned to go, they wanted to go, but the door was shut by Jesus himself. Ever happen to you?

When we pray for the will of God do we mean it or are we praying to try to bring God over to our way of thinking? We come to God with our list: Lord,

- I want to live in a small cozy little town with white picket fence,
- I want to attend a church that has only contemporary music.
- I want to work at a cute little boutique where I can get a good discount on their cute little clothes.
- I want to meet a man who makes a lot of money and who will be able to give me the cute little house with the picket fence.

So, my question is, do we really want God's will, or do we want Him to fulfill our wish list? I know this may be funny to read, but don't we often do this? As a pastor's wife I have.
"Father, I want your will more than anything so please:

- Send us to a church close to our family.
- Send us to a church in the country.
- Let us have a house close to, well no one."

Oh, I'm laughing as I write. Our children are scattered from Ohio to South Carolina to Florida. We live in the city and pastor a multiethnic church. Our home is in a neighborhood where the houses sit almost on top of each other. And oh, we love it. We have great neighbors; we have a wonderful congregation. God is blessing. The Spirit is present in our services. It feels so good to know we are where God led us.

God knows exactly what He is doing and when He said, "I have great plans for you for a great future full of hope," He meant it. And many times, He leads us to places and through circumstances we would never have imagined. He shuts doors to places that would destroy us, and He opens doors to places where we can grow and thrive. We can't put God in a box and try to constrain Him by telling Him what we want.

Today, surrender completely to His plan even if the direction He is leading seems completely different from what you envisioned. He loves you and He will never take you where His grace will not keep you.

I wonder what would have happened if God had given me what I wanted instead of leading us into His perfect will. Then again maybe I don't want to know because being in His will is the perfect place to be.

Prayer

Father,

Your will above all, even though I may have to lay aside my wants. You know what's best for me.

Help me to trust You even when I don't understand.

Give me the courage to go or stay at your word.

In Jesus' Name, Amen!

23

Keep Your Eyes on Jesus

I keep my eyes always on the LORD.
With him at my right hand, I will not be shaken.
Psalm 16:8

Often as I'm driving to the office, I will be moving along at a good clip (within the speed limit) and ahead, traffic has slowed to a crawl. I continue in bumper-to-bumper movement until I come upon the cause. No, it's not an accident. No one has been stopped for a violation. It is only a police car parked behind a construction vehicle. As soon as the cars in front of me understand the problem, they put the pedal to the metal and away we all go. As if there was anything they could do about it anyway!

It reminds me of life. Things are going well; we are growing in our walk with the Lord, and suddenly we get our eyes on something that slows us down. It is usually something little and many times it is something that isn't even our concern. Nevertheless, we are nosey and so we fix our sights on that one small issue and before we know it, we aren't looking to Jesus, We are looking at the problem.

Here's the thing: When we slow down, those who may not be as far along the road of faith as we are, may slow down as well.

"No man is an island entire of itself, "John Donne wrote. "Every man is a piece of the continent, a part of the main." As a part of the body of Christ, everything we do affects someone. That's why we must keep our eyes on Jesus. He knows the road. He's traveled it! He will take care of the roadwork!

Prayer

Father,

So many times I allow myself to become distracted by little things. And as I focus on them, they become big things that threaten to obscure the brightness of your presence.

Forgive me, Help me to look to you in spite of all the things that vie for my attention.

In Jesus' Name, Amen!

 Notes

24
Father Knows Best

"Father, if you are willing, please take this cup of suffering away from me. Yet I want your will to be done, not mine."
Luke 22:42

Nothing could have prepared Naomi for the heartache life would bring her as she married Elimelech. Like most brides, I'm sure she had stars in her eyes and was prepared to live out her dream with the man she loved.

Things went well for time. The couple had two boys. They named them Mahlon and Chilion. (I wonder how long Elimelech, and Naomi had to look in baby name books to find those two unique gems.)

Things happen as we all know and there was a famine in Bethehem-Judah where the little family lived, so Elimelech took his brood and moved to Moab.

After a time, Elimelech died, and Naomi found herself alone with her two sons. Eventually the boys found wives in the land that had become their home, but 10 years later, both of them died. Poor Naomi, living in a strange land. She had lost her husband and now her two sons. What unimaginable sorrow she must have felt! In one version of the Bible Naomi tells her daughters-in-law, "God has raised his fist against me." In other words, "I've been dealt a hard blow."

I'm sure many of us have been where Naomi was. We have suffered a terrible loss of some kind and we wonder what in the world God was thinking. Some of us may even get angry with God. The plain truth is this: Life is hard! Sometimes it can be almost unbearable. BUT we need to understand that God doesn't take delight in saying no to our requests or allowing our loved ones to be taken from us. It breaks His heart to see our hearts broken.

When our youngest son was taken from us, I wrote this in my journal, "When that which is best is also that which is hardest, our faith is sorely tried."

You see our Father always knows best. He is never taken by surprise, and He does all things well. As I traveled through the Valley of the Shadow of death with my son, I learned those valuable lessons.

When the smoke cleared, and the ashes cooled, I was able to think clearly, and the truth pierced my shattered heart, "God loved me. He was with me. He would never leave me. He would see me through." And He has. He does. And He will. He will do the same for you if you allow Him to.

Today, no matter what dark valley you travel through, God wants to bring joy on your journey, He wants to bring triumph from your tragedy, He wants to bring beauty from your ashes!

Prayer

Father,

Watching someone you love suffer and ultimately die, is hard. But wait, you know that. You watched as your Son was tortured and then killed. You understand, you care!

What freedom knowing that brings! Thank you for holding me when I cry, for being patient when I have questions, and for never giving up on me.

In Jesus loving Name, Amen!

25
Come!

Come to me, all of you who are weary
and carry heavy burdens,
and I will give you rest.
Matthew 11:28

I often overschedule myself. I put things on my calendar thinking I have "down time" arranged, and something will come up that is urgent, and well, I don't have a choice, I have to do it. There goes my time of relaxation and renewal. Before I know it, I'm in a state of upheaval and exhaustion. And you know what happens when you are exhausted?

Discouragement and negativity come a callin'. I have had moments of utter despair during these weary times.
The fact is the devil will kick you while you are down. He will make mountains out of mole hills, oceans out of puddles and towering infernos out of a spark. I just came through one of those times. I'll admit it, I was about to jump off the cliff of "what's the use" when the Lord, faithful Father that He is, reminded me I could find rest by spending some time with Him.

I always spend time in prayer and in the Word before I begin my day, but the reality of it is, it required more than just coming to God in prayer. I needed to sit on my Father's lap, snuggle up close to His heart, and spill all my frustration, my fatigue, my hurt, my longings and, I hate to admit it, my doubts!

There is nothing like just being held by the strong arms of a loving Father. I can tell Him things people would laugh at. I can cry, and He understands. And He always knows just what to whisper to my longing heart.

Are you weary today? Are the burdens you carry dragging you down? Why don't you take some time and just rest on the Fathers lap? There is nothing like a moment with the Master.

Prayer

Father,

Overextending ourselves is unavoidable sometimes and we find we are too tired to even think straight. Help us during those seasons, to come to You and be held, healed, and revived.

In Jesus' Name, Amen!

26
Keep Looking Up

I was driving into work one day and even though it was an overcast rather gloomy day, I looked up and saw the beautiful hills that surrounded me. Just beyond, the sky was arrayed in a beautiful pattern that could only have come from the imagination of God. He is a great artist, isn't He?

David said in Psalm 121:1 - *I lift up my eyes to the hills. From where does my help come? My help comes from the LORD, who made heaven and earth.*

Think about this: When we look to the hills, our eyes are drawn to the heavens. At least mine are. And in a day when we are tempted to become earth bound, I want to encourage you to head to the hills. In case you are more sophisticated, you may want to change that to "Ascend to the Mountain." Whatever your vernacular, we all need to go higher.

I love the beach, but I guess the Mountain Mama is in my blood, (I was, after all, born in Wild Wonderful West Virginia) because I feel so alive in the mountains. It's green, it's lush and it feels safe there.

David had confidence in God. He knew He couldn't face the giants in his life without God's help. And if we read about the life of David, we know he faced more than one giant. Am I right?

Do we have confidence in God? Do we believe IN God? Or do we believe God? There is a difference. Lots of folks believe in God. They believe that He exists, but they don't really believe Him.

We good Christian girls love to spout scripture, but do we really believe what is coming forth from us? I know

It's easy to exhort and proclaim "thus saith the Lord," but when we are in the nitty gritty of life and the storm is raging, do we believe God: when He promised

- He would never leave us,
- He promised to protect us.
- He would uphold us with His strong right arm.
- No weapon formed against us will prosper.
- We are the apple of His eye.

If we do believe His promises, then we will have peace even in

- the fiercest storms,
- the hottest battles and
- the deepest grief.

If we don't believe God nor believe what He says, we will find ourselves continually overwhelmed and under satisfied. What God says, He means. What He promises, He will do.

I don't know where you are in your journey, but if you find yourself discouraged and lacking hope. If you are in need of the refreshing wind of the Holy Spirit, you need to Head to the Hills. I encourage you to look up....there is a better day coming. Today could be that day.

Prayer

Father,

I remember my Uncle Ralph saying, "keep looking up." He knew that when we look down, we get down and discouraged. Help us to understand our help comes from above. Oh, it's sweet to trust You.

In Jesus' Name, Amen!

27
Go!

Go into all the world
And preach the Good News to everyone.
Mark 16:5

As long as this planet exists, there will be people who need Jesus. As the Children of God, we have been given the command to "go into all the world." We try to make excuses by saying, "I can't go all over the world. I'm not called to be a missionary." May I disagree with you? Yes, you are called to be a missionary.

I chuckled when I read some of the definitions for missionary. One of them is "campaigner." I laughed because most of the time we don't have any trouble getting on the bandwagon for our favorite politician. We will argue to the moon and back about who is the best person for the job. Most of the time we end up picking the lesser of two evils. And yet when it comes to crusading for Jesus, we become introverted and tongue-tied.

Let's face it. Most of us are terrified to talk about Jesus to a non-believer. I think perhaps it's because we talk about Him so infrequently to those who already believe. Think about it: We talk about our favorite sports teams, and we ladies love to talk about hair, clothes, and make-up.

There's nothing wrong with that. God wants us to enjoy our lives and have fun. But when it comes to sharing the good news, the challenge has been issued. Do it! It may be as simple as having a Sunday School class or Bible study in a fast-food restaurant. You might be surprised what kind of feedback you get from sitting together with a group of people and talking about Jesus. You don't have to approach someone and threaten hellfire if they don't know Jesus. They will hear the words you speak to each other; they will see the way you respect the wait staff; they will see the expressions on your face.

You might be surprised to know that when I have been involved in adventures such as this, people approach us. It's amazing how God steps into the middle of a group of obedient people.

People need the Lord. There isn't an option. Go get them!

Prayer

Father,

When I think about all the people, just in my circle of influence, who need Jesus, my heart is broken.

Help me, equip me, and lead me as I move among those who need your touch.

I know if I am obedient, you will go before me. Thank you, Jesus, Amen!

28
Be Ready!

You also must be ready all the time,
for the Son of Man will come.
when least expected.
Matthew 24:44

My daughter is the busy mama of three children, ages fourteen, fifteen and seventeen. Mornings can be chaotic, as you mamas well know. Sometimes my girl has been known to jump in the car in her nightgown or jammies to take her children to school. One morning had been particularly frenzied and so she didn't take time to put on what I call "street" clothes.

She successfully delivered the kiddoes to school and was almost at the entrance of her neighborhood, when she realized traffic was backed up. As she got closer, she saw their family dog, who apparently had followed her to the end of their road and had decided to wait on her in the middle of the busy highway.

Her husband was there, frantically trying to get said dog in the car. The dog wasn't having it. Megan jumped out of her car and ran to help her husband. Seeing reinforcements, he got back in his car and pretended to be an onlooker while Meg tried her best to persuade the stubborn dog to come get in her car. The best part, wait for it.....are you ready? There was a policeman there as well. Can you picture it? There is my daughter in all her natural glory. No makeup, hadn't brushed her teeth, and in her nightgown for all the world to see. Well, maybe not all the world, but you get the picture.

It was finally decided that Meg should get in her car and when she turned into their neighborhood, hopefully the dog would follow. And as it turns out, he did just that. The got home safely, and Meg didn't hit her husband in the head with a hammer. We laughed a long time about that adventure.

I said all that to say this. We need to be prepared and stay prepared for any eventuality. Every single time my house gets messed up, and I don't have time to tidy it, someone will drop by. And I am mortified. It pays to be ready!

You know where I'm going, right? Jesus is coming soon. We've been hearing that for as long as we have been on this earth. For generations, preachers have been exhorting us to be ready, teachers have been teaching us what to expect. And yet, I wonder, do we live our lives as though we really believe it? Is our heart house clean? Are all the cobwebs out of the corners? Are all the secret sins confessed and forgiven? Are we living daily in the presence of our Heavenly Father, feasting on His faithfulness, submerged in His Word, saturating ourselves in prayer?

It's easy to get slack as the days drag on, but the Bible tells us at a time when we LEAST expect it, Jesus will come. Will you be ready for that great and awful day, or like my daughter who was not prepared to make a public appearance, will you be caught unawares?

It's worth repeating: It pays to be ready! Eternity with Jesus is the reward! That should motivate us all.

Prayer

Father, so many times, I'm caught unprepared for things life brings to me, but I know I cannot neglect my preparation for Your return. Keep the promise and the reality of your coming upmost in my mind and help me to look forward to seeing you face to face and hearing the words, "Welcome home my good and faithful servant."

In Jesus' Name, Amen!

29
God is Always Good!

For the LORD is good.
His unfailing love continues forever,
and his faithfulness continues to each generation.
Psalm 100: 5

On September 11, 2001, we were going about our daily routines: Getting our kids off to school, dressing for work, planning our day. And suddenly our lives were forever changed. We would never feel safe again. We were abruptly made aware of our extreme vulnerability. We had been attacked on our own soil and if it could happen once, it might happen again. Our lives had been inexorably altered.

We now faced a new reality! For weeks we flew flags from our homes, our churches, even our cars. We attended prayer meetings, and we kept our children close. We questioned, we cried, we bombarded heaven with cries for help and understanding.

There were those who questioned why a God, who has the reputation of being good, could let this happen. We all struggled to make sense of a heinous, senseless act of malevolence.

No matter what happens, if we belong to God, we have peace because we know He is good. He is good when we aren't. He is good when wicked people plot their plans and strategize their schemes. He is good when circumstances aren't. It's who He is. He can't be anything but good! It is because of His great love for us that He allows each of us to make the choice to do good or to carry out evil. And when evil devises and fulfills its vision, good people often suffer. It's been that way since Adam and Eve sinned.

This side of eternity we will never understand. But in a world where change is inevitable and we are at the mercy of the whims of evil men, we can cling to the One Who Changes Not!

Whatever you are facing,
whatever your fears,
hold on tight!

Prayer

Father,

In a world that is always changing, I am thankful, you are still the same. You never change.

You will always be my Father, holding my hand, supporting me, assuring me of your presence even in the most confusing of times.

Thank you for your unfailing faithfulness.
In Jesus' beautiful Name, Amen!

30
Forgive and Move On!

Do not repay evil with evil or insult with insult.
On the contrary, repay evil with blessing, because to this you
were called
so that you may inherit a blessing.
I Peter 3:9

Do not repay evil with evil. I think it's crystal clear what the Bible is saying. Haven't we all read the words of Jesus, "Love your enemies, do good to those that hurt you?" And yet most of the time, when we have been offended, insulted, or injured, our first response is to "get back" at our perpetrator. Child of God, what are you thinking? That goes against the message of Jesus and the example He set.

I'm shaking my head because so many times we rush to "take sides" and make it our mission to destroy the person who started it all. I'm talking here about the Body of Christ, those who have been redeemed by the Blood, Christians who have been filled with the Spirit of God pitting themselves against each other for a cause! There should only be one side, God's side.

I think we forget who we are exactly and what is expected of us. Let me lay it out. We are the Family of God. We aren't supposed to act and react like those who don't know Jesus. We are supposed to love our enemies and find opportunities to do good to them.

Nowhere in the Word does it say we are to tear them down, run over them, and wipe them out. We are His children, the apple of His eye. All of us. Do we remember we are a chosen people, a royal priesthood, a holy nation, God's special possession? That's who and what we are and yet more often than not, we act like a gang of thugs! It's sad when a brother hurts another brother or sister affronts a sister. But it happens.

The key is to forgive, forget and move on. "Easier said than done!" you say. Maybe, but it's not an option. I heard someone say once that the wilderness was just a passing through place for the Israelites and yet many of them were buried in the desert. It is not God's plan for His people to be buried in the Wilderness of Resentment! It is His will for us to pass through it into the beautiful plan He has for us. Life is too short to carry a grudge. It will make you physically, emotionally, and spiritually sick. It will separate you from joy and peace and keep you from walking in victory.

Today, give the burden to Jesus, lay it at His feet, and leave it there. Stop fighting and trying to convince anyone and everyone that your way, your plan, your idea is the only one. You are wasting precious time that should be spent doing positive things IN and FOR the Kingdom of God.

Prayer

Father,

I do want your will. Sometimes I want something so much, I forget to consult you and I push my own agenda.

Please forgive me. And if I have offended anyone, give me the courage to walk in obedience and ask for their forgiveness.

And Father, help me to be willing to forgive those who don't always agree with me; they are your children, too.

In Jesus Name.
Amen!

31
Choose to Let Go!

Make allowance for each other's faults
and forgive anyone who offends you.
Remember the Lord forgave you,
so you must forgive others.
Colossians 3:13

Why do we want to hang on to things that hurt us? Why do we rehearse and rehash the wrongs done to us? Why, after we THOUGHT we had let it go, do we dig deep to excavate the very things we KNOW will bring us down?

I was struggling with an issue one day, and I found myself reliving a hurt and becoming frustrated; and even more than that, confused! And I WAS bewildered, perplexed and my mind was in chaos. The spirit of God reminded me, "Confusion doesn't come from Me."

God was doing great things in us and around us. His blessings were being poured out. Why was I even giving this "affront" a second thought? You know I was a willful child and my mama often had to apply the board of education to my seat of learning. I smile ruefully because God does the same thing. He doesn't hold back when it comes to disciplining a stubborn child. And He was "in my face" with the truth of what was taking place in my life.

Here's what I know: The devil will do his best to make us overlook all the wonderful things in our lives and turn our attention to things that will take our focus away from the here and now! He is a liar and yet in our weakness, we somehow allow him to convince us what he is telling us is factual.

I found myself duped by the devil, and when I realized what I was allowing him to do, this sister got up on her holy high horse. No sir, no ma'am, I was DONE! He was not going to make me lose my joy over something I had dragged into the present from the distant past. I was not going to live in that shame!

Right now, I am a Child of God, blessed by His Almighty Hand, enjoying Kingdom dwelling, and there is no room in my heart or my mind for self-deprecation instigated by something which should have been forgiven and forgotten a long time ago. I made a decision. I was not going to think about this offense. I chose to let it go.

When the devil brings it to mind, I'll do just what Jesus did and quote scripture at him. Scripture is a powerful repellent against the wiles of Satan. He can't stand it, and he can't stand up under it. Satan has no control over who I am, or what I think. I will rise up and walk in forgiveness and victory! I did; and what a change I experienced.

Today, don't waste time and energy carrying a grudge, let it go. Give it to Jesus. He knows exactly how to handle it.

Prayer

Father,

Today, I'm so weary from holding on to this heavy load. The fact is, I can't seem to get over this hurt. Help me! Right now, I choose to let go of what is holding me captive. It's hurting my witness, it's hurting my relationships, it's hurting me. Here it is! Thank you for helping me to rid myself of something that was only causing me pain.

I love you and each day I will choose to keep my hands off of this thing that has kept me from moving on.

In Jesus' Name, Amen!

32
When We Don't Understand

As you do not know the path of the wind,
or how the body is formed in a mother's womb,
so you cannot understand the work of God,
the Maker of all things.
Ecclesiastes 11:5

Why is it that we don't want something until we get overlooked for the thing we thought we didn't want? I know that's a convoluted question! I am shaking my head even as I write.

I found myself in a situation somewhat like the aforementioned. (Sorry, I used to work for attorneys and these words come to the fore occasionally!) I really didn't want to put myself "out there," but I was asked to do so and couldn't bring myself to oblige. I was in a quandary. The timing was ok, but not perfect. Still, when an opportunity presents itself, we often feel the need to pursue it until God either opens or shuts a door. What should I do? So, I prayed and asked the Lord to show me in a specific way if I was do this thing. I forgot about it and then my specific prayer got a specific answer. Do it! I prayed; other people prayed that God's will would be done as I proceeded.

Wait for it! It didn't come to fruition. Part of me was so relieved I didn't know what to do. I confess I was not 100 percent invested in this venture. However, I began to question the whys and the wherefores! You'd think I'd learn when God says "no" to just let that be that. But oh no, not me. I wallowed it around in my heart and mind trying to figure out where everything went wrong. Why had God given me the sign to pursue this avenue, or was it in fact, God, or just me?

God has ways of teaching us obedience and sometimes they are, shall we say, unusual? As I struggled with my feelings of offense and inadequacy, God in his loving kindness taught me so much about mercy and grace. He put me in a place where I had to get on board with the plan without actually being a part of it. He put people in my path that needed encouragement about the very thing from which I had been omitted! I either had to come to a place of complete surrender or wallow in the mud. And so, I encouraged and recommended and as I did, all those negative feelings went the way of the wind.

Looking back, I see my Father's hand in it all. He knew I needed to learn some things. And He always knows just the right way to teach us the hard lessons of life. I firmly believe He orchestrated it all. Through this "adventure," I learned so much about obedience, faith, and dependence on the One Who knows me best! I'm thankful!

Prayer

Father,

Many times, most of the time in fact, we don't understand your ways.

When we don't understand, we need to trust you. After all, you do all things well.

As the old song says, "I don't need to understand, I just need to hold your hand." I am, and I will.

In Jesus' Name, Amen!

33
I Am His!

But now, thus says the Lord, your Creator, O Jacob,
And He who formed you, O Israel,
Do not fear, for I have redeemed you.
I have called you by name; you are Mine!
Isaiah 43:1

"I am Yours and You are mine." Those are the words I heard when I tuned in to my favorite station for the drive to the office today. Those seven words plowed their way into the depths of my soul and found purchase there. They reverberated with meaning and feeling and truth. I belong to God. I am His child. And it gets better, He belongs to me! He is my Father. Mine!

The one who created the earth, the skies, the seas, and me! Can our minds even begin to contemplate what that entails? Everything He has is available to me if I walk humbly and obediently before Him. To put it simply, "the sky is the limit!"

Wait, looking at it through the lens of the eternal, "there is no limit, not even the sky" because someday, the sky will not limit us from entering the gates of a place dreams are made of. The other day someone said, "I'm not good FOR anything. I am not good AT anything." I replied, "You are a child of God, now raise your right hand and say, 'I know who I am in Christ.' As children of the King of the Universe, we need only to read His "love letter" to us. I find there the truth of my inheritance. I am chosen, I'm royalty, I am part of the kingdom.

I am God's own possession. I am the apple of His eye! I could keep this up all day! It doesn't matter what others think of me, if I am overlooked, ignored, misunderstood, or unappreciated. I am a child of the King!

Today, look up and revel in the fact you are His and He is yours! The very truth of that glorious reminder brings with it joy unspeakable and full of glory.

Prayer

Father,

I know who I am. I am your child, forgiven because of what Jesus did on the cross.

Help me never to forget that my position in the Family of God was bought and paid for.

Forgive me when I allow Satan or others to make me feel less than I know I am.

I love you.

In Jesus' Name, Amen!

34

Brighten the Corner

Let your light shine before men ...
Matthew 5:16

Do you find yourself backed in a corner filled with despair and negativity? Are the people around you pessimistic and miserable? Are their words filled with gloom and doom? Have you ever thought God may have placed you there to bring light to that dark corner?

I know the temptation is to launch into a sermon or a dissertation of everything that is wrong in their lives. I talked to someone one day who said they had been going through a very difficult time: car broke down, furnace went out in the house, one thing after the other. She worked with a "Christian" who said, "The reason you are having so much trouble is because you are 'living in sin." I was appalled. When mercy should have been extended judgment was tendered.

I know the heart of Jesus was broken because one who called themselves His offered condemnation instead of compassion. As Christians, as children of the light, as the image of the very Light of the World, we can't meld into the blend of bitterness and blight. When we walk into the murkiness of a corner where pain and hopelessness hold their victims hostage, we bring with us a glimmer of hope and a foretaste of the peace that has been promised by our loving Father, not a legalistic sense of our own righteousness.

I want to clarify; I'm not suggesting we approve of sin. I am suggesting we love as Jesus did and allow the Holy Spirit to do His job, which incidentally He does very well. Do we need to be reminded we are carriers of the light and messengers of grace? Have we forgotten the grace and mercy extended to us in our deepest darkest night of the soul? It's time for us to pay it forward and offer some grace and mercy to others who so need the healing power of Jesus in their souls.

Prayer

Father,

Forgive me when I have been full of judgment instead of full of grace.

Help me to offer hope, to shine the light of Jesus into the dark corners of sin.

Help me to remember where I was when you found me and use that memory to be a blessing to the one who needs it most.

In Jesus' Name, Amen!

35
I Know Who I Am

But you are a chosen people,
a royal priesthood, a holy nation,
God's special possession,
that you may declare the praises of Him
who called you out of darkness
into his wonderful light.

I Peter 2:9

I used to do ministry with a group of people who teased me A LOT about being an airhead or blonde, you know those jokes! And every time they did, I raised my right hand and said, "I know who I am in Christ." You see it doesn't matter what people think you are, or what they TRY to make you think you are, if you know who you are in Christ, it rolls off you like water off a duck's back

Do you know WHO you are in Christ? Do you know WHAT you are in Christ? The Bible clearly tells us we have been chosen by God. Do you understand what that means? It means the Creator of the Universe looked at you and saw something of value. You are worth so much to Him that He sent Jesus, long before you were even a twinkle in someone's eye, to die for you, to pay the price for your sins. You see, He knew you could never afford the cost of your redemption and so He willingly paid it for you! He chose you and when you accepted His call to come and be forgiven, He made you holy and righteous. His holiness, his righteousness....not yours!!!

Are you feeling pretty good about yourself and what Jesus has done? Well, you should be, because that's not all. You are a part of a holy nation. You are related to all the redeemed through the blood of Jesus. And oh, I love this, we are a Royal Priesthood! You are royalty....you are somebody!

So right now, raise your right hand and say, "I KNOW who I am in Christ." Go ahead, try it!

PRAYER

Father, when people mock me and the enemy accuses me help me to remember who I am in Christ Jesus.

In His Name,

Amen!

36
Wait!

For God alone, O my soul,
wait in silence, for my hope is from Him.
Psalm 62:5

Lazarus is sick. It looks serious. Mary and Martha, in their concern, send for Jesus. Now here's where the story gets interesting. The Bible tells us, "Jesus loved Mary, Martha, and Lazarus. When He heard Lazarus was sick, He stayed where He was for two more days." Wait, what? I mean I know how this story ends and I still sit with my mouth open in dismay! Jesus, you love Lazarus, he's really sick and you just stay put and do nothing? Yes, indeed! For sure! Absolutely! Then on the third day He said to his disciples, "Let's go, boys!" And off they went.

Jesus knows Lazarus is dead and buried before Mary and Martha tell Him. And in His spirit, He is filled with joy and excitement because He knows He is about to rock their world. Still when He came to the tomb the Bible tells us He wept! Oh, He wasn't weeping over Lazarus, He knew Lazarus would live again in a few minutes. Here's the thing I think we often miss in this story: Even though Jesus would bring glory to God through the miracle He was about to perform, it broke His heart to see Mary and Martha's sorrow. Have you ever stopped to think about that? Soon Mary and Martha's grief turned to joy because Jesus always has the last word. Lazarus came out of the tomb alive and well.

Sometimes Jesus sees fit to make us wait. We think all is lost. We wonder where He is and why He doesn't come post haste to rescue us. Remember what He said to the disciples? "This sickness won't end in death." And it didn't. Yes, Lazarus died, but that wasn't the end! Praise the Lord!

Wherever you are today, whatever you are waiting for, be encouraged. Jesus isn't finished yet! He has planned a wonderful finale for you! It will be for your good and to bring glory to himself. I promise you, it's worth the wait!

Prayer

Father,
Oh my, it's hard to wait.
But as we wait, you are working.
And while I wait, I will worship.
I know that you have something good for me.
I praise you for always knowing what I need, when I need it and how to provide what I need.
In Jesus' Name,
Amen!

37
Closed Doors

Now when they had gone through Phrygia
and the region of Galatia,
they were forbidden by the Holy Spirit
to preach the word in Asia.
After they had come to Mysia,
they tried to go into Bithynia,
but the Spirit did not permit them.
Acts 16:6-7

How many times do we head in a certain direction only to have the door shut firmly on our plans? This scripture tells us the apostles experienced it more than once. Do you notice they didn't argue? They just followed where the Spirit of God led them? How about you and me? Are we as compliant and consecrated in obeying the voice of God as these holy men of God? I'm reminded of the one big thing I learned from engaging in the Bible Study "Experiencing God." To me the words are so profound, "Look to see where God is working and join Him there."

If God shuts a door in one area, He most certainly has opened another for you to go through. Look what happened to the apostles. God had been working in Macedonia and preparing the way for the apostles. When they arrived, they met Lydia, a seller of purple, at a prayer meeting. The Bible says, "her heart was opened" and she and her household were baptized. Wow! Who would have thought? Oh, but God wasn't finished with them. The apostles made a sorcerer mad because they cast a demon out of their main money maker and they were beaten and thrown in prison.

Paul and Silas didn't know it, but they had just been thrown through another door God had opened. There in that slimy, stinky jail, they sang hymns and praised God. And the Lord honored their praise and caused an earthquake. As a result, the Philippian jailer and his whole family were saved and baptized, then they gave first aid to the apostles.

What would have happened if those mighty men of God hadn't obeyed the voice of the Spirit? We know at least two families who might never have heard the gospel message and a demon-possessed slave who might not have ever known freedom. What a lesson for us today! The next time God closes a door, look for the one He has opened instead and walk boldly through it! You will see God at work! Join him there!

Prayer

Father,

How often pride in my own abilities raises its ugly head and I think I know the best path to take. And then I have run into more trouble than I could handle.

Help me to learn from those mistakes and trust you to lead me exactly where you want me to go.

Lead me, Jesus. I will gladly follow you.

In your sweet Name,

Amen!

38
Let it Rain

Then they cried out to the LORD in their trouble,
and He brought them out of their distress.
He stilled the storm to a whisper;
the waves of the sea were hushed.
They were glad when it grew calm,
and He guided them to their desired haven.
Psalm 107:28-31

I had created a little oasis on my porch with delicate flowers and beautiful greenery. Then the storm hit. The rain was torrential, pummeling my little flowers mercilessly. The next morning, they seemed haggard and done in. Something miraculous happened! The sun appeared, and those little drenched blossoms raised their tiny heads to the source of light and in a few hours, they were their perky selves again.

Life is like that. Storms come, and rains beat down on us in a seemingly unending torrential downpour. Sometimes it rains so hard you can't see what is right in front of you. Oh, but one day, Jesus says, "enough," and as we raise our heads to the Son, the light begins to dawn. The storm we just survived was as needful as the brightness of the noon day sun.

Flowers can't grow without rain, and neither can we. Just as the flowers are strengthened and nourished by the rain so are we. Because it is during the darkness of the storm that we learn to trust Jesus as never before. We trust Him to bring us safely through when lightning flashes and thunder crashes. Has He ever failed to bring us through? No, and He never will.

The next time you are in the midst of a life storm, remember, the sun will shine again, and your life will begin to bloom with the fragrance of the grace of God.

Prayer

Father,

Looking back, I can see your hand in the storm. I'm thankful for the rain, because it caused me to grow as I rested safely in the palm of your hand.

I love you.

In your sweet name,

Amen!

39
God's Plan is Best

The heart of man plans his way,
but the Lord establishes his steps.
Proverbs16:9

Ever have a plan go awry? I have. Ever had something you THOUGHT you wanted but you were pretty sure it wasn't what God wanted for you? You know what I mean don't you? You pray for God to shut every door you aren't supposed to go through and when He shuts them firmly in your face. No doubt about it, no question the answer is a resounding NO, yet you find yourself filled with emotions you can't name.

I once found myself in that very place. I had prayed for God's will, and I truly and sincerely wanted what He wanted. The prospect presented was one I wasn't fully convinced was right for me. I had doubts, I was conflicted, and yet what if?

The reality is, God had a better plan. When I realized that, I praised Him for His wisdom, and I thanked Him for the answer to prayer. I would like to say that's the end of it, but unfortunately or maybe not so unfortunately it wasn't over yet.

As I went through my day, I wasn't experiencing the peace I thought I would. I was struggling. As I was driving home, I started to pray, "Father, I have this little niggling feeling that I can't name. It's deep in my spirit, help me to identify it because I want your peace to fill me over the resolution of this situation." And then from the depths of my spirit, my words began to flow. "I'm feeling a little embarrassed, I'm a little indignant, throw in a little bit of the dog in the manger syndrome, I'm a little jealous, I'm hurt, I'm offended and Father, I don't want to feel any of those things. Please empty me of everything and give me a fresh anointing. You are always right; and to tell the truth, I only started this because someone else suggested it." And peace came, and peace has stayed. No more doubts, no more feelings of inadequacy, no more questions. God has spoken and like Mary, I say, "May it be as You have said." There is nothing, and I mean nothing, like being in the center of the divine will of a Holy God!

Prayer

Oh, Lord,

Sometimes I let people convince me of what I need to do. When I listen and realize I'm in the wrong place, help me to admit it, repent, and get back in the center of Your will for my life. It's the best place to be.

In Jesus' Name, Amen!

40
Keep Your Guard Up

"The devil can't MAKE us do anything," said a very wise woman. I stopped for a minute to think about it. And you know what? It's true. While it's true he knows which buttons to push and it's also true he has a whole arsenal of temptations to throw at us, he can't actually FORCE us to yield to him and his evil plans. In I Peter 5:8 we are warned: Watch out for your great enemy, the devil. He prowls around like a roaring lion, looking for someone to devour.

Can't you just see him slinking in the darkness, hiding in the shadows, lurking just around the corner? He will tempt us to yield to discouragement. He will make our circumstances seem impossible. He will whisper chaotic thoughts to us. And if that fails, he comes to us looking like an angel, making sin look so inviting and so, well, right.

We must keep our guard up all the time. We need to be constantly aware of his tricks. We are commanded to brandish the sword of the spirit. We are urged to pray without ceasing.
It is Satan's goal to steal, kill and destroy. It's his only goal. Even the strongest saint ought to be wary of his antics. He is the father of lies, he is the perpetrator of doubt, he is the author of discouragement.

The picture I paint is a chilling one. Think on this. We don't have to give in to him. He is a great big bully, but he can be stopped by speaking the beautiful Name of our bountiful Savior.

The most victorious Christians I know are the ones who have hidden the WORD of God in their hearts and who spend copious amounts of time on their knees. They have found the secret to staying strong against the devil and his wiles. They know, and the devil knows as well, he is no match for a saint of God who can wield the sword of truth and who fights on their knees.

Prayer

Father,

Help me to remember I have power over Satan and not only that, but your Word tells me I have power over his power. That gives me the confidence I need to stand firm.

Thank you, Jesus!

In your sweet name,

Amen!

41
You Can Trust Jesus

Trust in the Lord with all your heart,
and do not lean on your own understanding.
Proverbs 3:5

Oh, the confusion, the frustration, the angst when you put yourself "out there" and you feel like a door is slammed in your face. It can be embarrassing, and the devil will use it to make you feel less than worthy.

Let's just be real. He will make it seem that others see you as incapable, you know, just not good enough. The temptation to allow your soul to sink deep into doubts about your abilities and your value is powerful.

Ask yourself, "Didn't I pray for God to show me His perfect will? Didn't I actually ask Him to shut every door firmly in my face if it wasn't in His plan for me?" The answer comes back "yes, I did indeed." But another question arises, "Did I mean it?"

At the time I'm sure we all mean it when we tell God we want His will no matter what. That's when we have hope that what we want will in fact be His will. But when He makes it plain that He is leading in another direction, well that's a different story.

What we all need to remember is how very much we are loved by the Father. We need to be reminded of His words from Jeremiah 29:11-13 - For I know the plans I have for you, declares the LORD, plans to prosper you and not to harm you, plans to give you hope and a future. Then you will call on me and come and pray to me, and I will listen to you. You will seek me and find me when you seek me with all your heart.

When the thing we think we wanted more than anything is suddenly gone, God is still very present with His very own plan. And it's a good plan. It's so much better than our plan. And He tells us if we seek Him with our whole heart, we will find Him. In other words, in due time, the perfect plan for your life and mine will be revealed. And one day, we will look back and see that His way is always the best way.

Prayer

Father,
When will I learn?

Help me to remember how sweet it is to trust You when I'm not sure of the way and even when I am.

Thank you for always working in my life for my good and for your glory.

In Jesus' name,
Amen!

42
Have Faith

Faith is the confidence
that what we hope for will actually happen;
it gives us assurance about things we cannot see.
Hebrews 11:1

Faith. What a great word! People write songs about it, preach about it, and even name their kids after it! But do we really operate in it?

Faith is the opposite of fear. Faith is the opposite of doubt. Faith activates the power of God in our lives, Fear gives Satan access to our hearts.

The Bible tells us we can't please God without Faith and yet many of us walk around from day to day always worried about something. In fact, when we aren't worried about something, we're worried that we aren't worried. You might chuckle at that, but it's true.

There are some people who love to worry. The story is told of someone who was trying to bring encouragement to a chronic worrier. They quoted scripture, they prayed, they tried to speak positively into a life dedicated to negativity. They went to visit one day trying to cheer the poor pessimist. Their words brought this response, "Leave me alone, I like to worry."

Now I don't think anyone LIKES to worry, but sometimes our failure to put our little hand in the great big hand of our omnipotent Father makes it look like we do. Of course, we will have times when we are tempted to fear and doubt, but as Children of God, we know God has commanded us to come to Him when fear tries to take root in our souls.

He has promised He will give us peace beyond what we could ever imagine! The truth is: we don't have to worry! The minute worry and doubt knock at your heart's door, run to

Jesus! He will send worry and doubt on their way as soon as we speak His Holy Name.

Prayer

Father,

Help me not to worry. When I'm tempted, remind me that worry doesn't accomplish anything except to keep me awake at night.

Trusting You is so much sweeter and that will bring Your power into action on my behalf.

I'm glad I'm yours.

In Jesus' Name,

Amen!

43
When You Don't Know What to Do!

We do not know what to do,
but we are looking
to you for help.
II Chronicles 20:12

I often get deep into II Chronicles 20. It is one of my favorite chapters in the entire Bible. In the opening verses, Jehoshaphat is in a pickle. He has just been informed that not one, but three armies are marching against Jerusalem.

Jehoshaphat was king, but he was human, and he was scared out of his wits. That's my translation. Wouldn't you be terrified? I know I would be. Jehoshaphat didn't just stand around quaking and shaking, he sprang into action, not on the battlefield, but in the prayer room. He called his people together, ordered a fast and they had a prayer meeting.

Jehoshaphat didn't call a meeting of the Defense Department, instead he took the threat to God, because he knew he couldn't win the battle with the resources he had. He knew he and his people didn't have a chance of coming out of this mess alive. So, he went to the One who could handle the invading armies. Now we know God already knew the issue and He had planned the deliverance before the invading armies ever left home.

Prayer is so much more than presenting our need to God. It is offering ourselves in total submission and trust to the God who is able. One of my favorite verses in this chapter is verse twelve. After Jehoshaphat took the details to the Lord, he ended by saying, "and we don't know what to do, but our eyes are on you." In other words, "Lord, we don't have the resources or the power to fight these armies and win, in fact, we don't have a clue as to what we are going to do. However, we know You know exactly what is happening and how to deliver us." And God did. And the people didn't have to lift their hands to fight.

I remember one day we were singing Where Could I Go but to The Lord. When we finished my sweet mama said, "Where would we want to go, but to the Lord?" And as His children, it should be our first response instead of our last resort. Today, you may be up against some difficult circumstances. You don't have any idea how to extricate yourself from the mess you're in. Take heart! Your Father knows. And when you yield yourself to Him, confessing you are helpless, He will step in and rescue you. Nothing is too hard for Him!

Prayer

Father,

Today, I am in a hard spot. I have tried to figure a way out, but I still don't have any idea as to what I should do. So, I give the matter to You.

I relinquish it into Your big, strong, almighty hands. I trust You to make a way where there seems to be no way. In Jesus Name, Amen!

44
Give the Reins to Jesus

He cared for them with a true heart
and led them with skillful hands.
Psalm 78:72

Recently on a visit to one of our favorite places on earth, Camden, South Carolina, we were blessed to attend our granddaughter Coley's horseback riding lessons. We watched with pride as she walked, trotted, and cantered her horse, Misty, and then she began jumping hurdles. Oh, this Nana's heart soared as I watched our sweet baby control that big old horse.

Later as we were driving home, we were discussing the other riders and horses that were participating in lessons along with Coley. She said, "Nannie, one of those horses in the ring today didn't have any eyes."

"What did you say, baby?" I gasped; not sure I heard her correctly.

She went on to tell me the horse had contracted an infection in his eyes and they both had to be removed. She said, "Really, he does much better now, because he was trying to see through all that infection in his eyes and it was affecting his performance."

I pondered! I thought back how each of the horses looked amazing as they were put through their paces. Frankly, I would be hard pressed to begin to figure out which one was blind. But how in the world did that horse navigate the obstacle course and clear the hurdles when he had no idea of where he was going?

As my mind tried to come to grips with what I had seen and what I now knew about that horse, a great spiritual truth was born in my spirit. The horse had no idea where he was

95

going, but the one who held the reins knew. The horse trusted his rider and as he was obedient to the slightest touch of the reins, he was able without any problem to sail over or walk around the obstacles placed in his way.

Tears fill my eyes as I marvel at this beautiful revelation. Sometimes God leads us into the unknown. We don't know where we are headed or what we will face as we go, but we can be sure of this one thing. God knows exactly where we are going. He holds the reins of our lives and as we are sensitive to His slightest tug on our spirit, we will overcome even the biggest boulders we encounter. We don't have to see to believe or to accomplish great things for God, we only have to trust and obey, and His skillful hands will guide us.

Prayer

Father,

How often you ask us to trust You as we walk blindly into situations we know nothing of.

Many times, we don't understand why You have even led us there.

Help us to trust You. Nothing surprises You. You know every hole in the road, every obstacle, and every rocky place.

Help us to obey every nuance of Your tug upon our hearts. Help us to trust You with every fiber of our being.

As we do, we know You will bring us to the place you have ordained for us.

In Jesus' Name, Amen!

45
Follow Where He Leads

In all your ways acknowledge Him and
He will direct your steps.
Proverbs 3:6

We make decisions every day. What will I wear to work? Should I pack my lunch or go out? Some decisions are more important than others. Some can be life changing. Should I change jobs? Should I accept more responsibility?

God has a perfect plan for our lives. Sometimes He doesn't share those plans with us right away. But He doesn't say, "I have something for you to do, guess what it is?" He is Good and He will make His plans known to us on a "need to know" basis. Sometimes we have to wait for weeks, months or even years.

During those long days with no revelation, we can become impatient, bored, and restless. The temptation to take matters into our own hands is almost overwhelming. I know; I can say, "Been there, done that more than once." I have pushed God aside and jumped ahead of Him and nearly ruined my life in the process.

God isn't just sitting on His throne listening to the heavenly choir sing! On second thought He probably is, but you and I know He can do more than one thing at a time, right? Even now He is moving people and circumstances into position and when everything is just right, He will show you the next step to take.

Don't ruin His surprise by stepping out on your own path instead of sitting still in His presence.

Prayer

Father,

How well do I know the consequences of depending on myself and my plans instead of committing myself and my way to You. From this moment on, I will wait on you, and I will follow only where you lead.

In Jesus' Name, Amen!

46
Power Promised

I will give you power
over all the power of the enemy and nothing
shall by any means harm you.
Luke 10:19

In the first part of that verse the promise is that we will have power to trample on snakes and scorpions. The apostle Paul was bitten by a viper and those around fully expected he would die. He didn't. I believe God can do the same thing today. Do we need to go around handling snakes and stepping barefoot on poisonous insects just to prove a point? Absolutely not! But the point is, we are promised that kind of power. And sometimes we run into vipers and scorpions of the human variety. The same thing applies. We have the power. But most of the time we don't act like it. We are so afraid people will think we are weird. And to the world we are weird.

- We believe that a man died for our sins, rose from the grave and is coming back again.
- We believe we can have a personal relationship with Him, and that we can communicate with Him through prayer, and He hears us.
- We believe the voice of the Holy Spirit speaks to us to guide us.

I mean if you think about it, that sounds a little crazy if you haven't met Jesus. Satan has no authority over us. He once did, but when we met Jesus, everything changed. We not only have power over him, but we also have power over his power. Think about it. I pray today the truth of that fact will infiltrate your heart with dynamite!

99

Satan has no hold on us. Let him do his worst, He can't separate us from God or His love. We are the anointed children of a Heavenly Father. We need to live like it. Claim your power today!

Prayer

Father,

Help me to remember who I am and whose I am. I claim the authority given to me as your child. I belong to you. Satan has no hold on me now.

Thank you, Jesus! Amen!

47
There's Power in the Pause

They that wait upon the Lord
shall renew their strength; they shall
mount up with wings as eagles,
they shall run and not grow weary,
they shall walk and not faint.
Isaiah 40:31.

I woke up one morning with the above scripture imbedded in my mind. It came to me that there are treasures to be found in the waiting. As we wait upon God, we are strengthened in our spirits. It stretches our spiritual muscles to wait. We often struggle and strain to find answers, instead of simply waiting in quietness of spirit for God to make His will known.

Sometimes it takes more strength to stand still than it does to act. There is peace to be found in the postponing. As we surrender ourselves to the Spirit of God and allow Him to satisfy us in the place where we are, peace will fill our hearts along with a deep knowing that His purpose is to make us more like Jesus.

There is power to be found in the pause. God wants us to be equipped with power. Power for us to use every difficult circumstance for His glory. Can you imagine the stories you will be able to share of the day-to-day power, peace, and presence of God you experienced as you waited for God to answer prayer?

Are you aware that there are others in the same place of discouragement and dismay who need to hear your story of triumph in the trial? Oh yes, this is a precious time, even though it seems endless. In these moments of helplessness, you only need to surrender to the Helper who Jesus promised would bring us comfort. Allow Him to work while you wait. Worship while you wait. Witness while you wait. Waiting time is never wasted time!

Prayer

Father,

Thank You for teaching me deep lessons of faith in my time of waiting.

Thank you for always being willing to walk with me through these times. I'm so glad I belong to you.

In Jesus' Name,

Amen!

48
Looking for Something New?

Behold, I will do a new thing.
Now it shall spring forth; Shall you not know it?
I will even make a road in the wilderness
And rivers in the desert.
Isaiah 43:19:

    I love this precious promise from the Living Word of the Eternal God. He is saying "Are you ready? I'm about to do something new and impossible!" A road in the wilderness? Rivers in the desert? Are you even kidding me? We all know the wilderness is a forsaken place and the desert is dry and full of sand and cacti. There are no rivers there, maybe an oasis once in a while. Ah, but God! He is able, and He is willing to do something extreme for those of us who are like withered plants. Are you wandering in the wilderness, confused, and directionally challenged? You want God's will in your life, but at this point in time, you don't have a clue what that is! He wants
to make your path plain, your crooked paths straight.

    He has promised to fashion a road where there is no road, and that road will be obvious to you. The way you are to take and the road you will travel will be made so clear to you there will be doubt as to your direction. If you follow him in obedience and faith, you will not lose your way or be sidetracked by the enemy.

    Are you in a desert place, parched, and in need of the Living Water? He has promised to provide a river in the barren wasteland in which you find yourself. A river with cool clear water to satisfy the thirsting of your dry, desperate soul!

Run to Him, He is the River, He is the Living Water. Only a drink from the well that never runs dry will quench the thirst burning deep within.

Whether you are wandering in the wilderness or desperate for a drink, God wants to do something new for you! He promised!!!!!

Prayer

Father,

I hunger and thirst for you. I submit myself to you to do a new thing in my life. Prepare me to walk in the plan you have for me.

In Jesus' Name, Amen!

49
Don't be Afraid

For God has not given us a spirit of fear,
but of power, and of love
and of a sound mind.
II Timothy 2:7

Fear is a terrible tangible thing. It can trap us in its tentacles and hold us there. It can become such a part of us that we are unable to function. Fear can convince us there is no hope. It can suggest to us that we have a dread disease and before we know we have all the symptoms. Fear can persuade us that everyone is against us. Fear can make us afraid to live our lives to the fullest.

Fear is not prejudiced. It just moves in whenever an opening appears. And when we give it an inch it takes a mile.

Did you know that fear is absolutely forbidden in the Bible? Jesus himself told us, "Don't let your hearts be troubled and don't let them be afraid." I don't think He was making a little suggestion. He meant what He said.

I was talking to someone the other day and they said they didn't want their children to have children because of the world we live in today. I understand that. I pray for the protection of my grandchildren every day. I pray they will not be blinded by sin and tricked into believing the lies the devil wants to tell them. You know, the world has always been a mess. From the moment man sinned, wickedness thrived. Then people sinned in secret, today they are openly flaunting their disobedience in the face of God. We don't have to be afraid; God is still in control. He lives, He rules, He reigns. I love the song that says, "No matter what happens He will care for me." He has promised to take care of us. He holds us in the palm of His almighty right hand. Our names are engraved there.

Fear is the opposite of faith. Fear opens us up to let the devil make us think there is no hope, and no one has a chance. You know He is a liar and the father of all lies, right? Then why should we be afraid? We are children of the King. We are overcomers because of WHO we are in Christ! Take heart, Trust Him! Let faith replace fear!

Prayer

Father,

The world is a scary place. We shake our heads when we think of the direction it is going. Help us not to dwell on the negatives, but to look to you – the only hope for us and the world. Turn our fear into faith.

You promised to never leave us. Help us to hold tight to that promise, to rebuke the lies of Satan, and to give us the strength to stand in the power that is ours.

In Jesus' mighty name! Amen!!

50
Resurrection Power

The Spirit of God,
who raised Jesus from the dead, lives in you.
And just as God raised Christ Jesus from the dead,
He will give life to your mortal bodies by this same Spirit
living within you.
Romans 8:11

I'm glad to be a child of God. My Father is Almighty. He is power. I tried to think of something to compare to the power of God, but His power is incomparable.

- Power means Control: No matter how things look, God is in control.
- Power means, supremacy: God is the greatest, the absolute, the ultimate
- Power means strength: God is the strongest.
- Power means ability: God can do anything.

I have felt like a ship that has been battered and my sails torn. I know you all have felt that way, too. But the good news is as my good friend songwriter Lawrence Chewning wrote, "The anchor holds in spite of the storm."

And today, as children of God we need to be reminded that we have power. Not just any kind of power, but resurrection power. We need to stand up and say, "We will stand on the Rock that never crumbles! We will trust Jesus who never fails! And no matter what the devil throws our way, we will walk in victory!"

In everything that happens in life there are lessons to be learned. Whether we learn them or not depends upon what our focus is. We can zero in on the circumstances around us, or we can focus on the awesome power of God Almighty to help us to overcome life's troubles and live in victory and power.

Either we will learn to be overcomers by faith, or we will continually live in defeat, with lives full of worry and fear about everything that comes our way. Christians should live above worry and fear because we should trust God.

Trust Him when we don't understand. Trust Him when all around us circumstances tempt us to throw up our hands and give up.

Today we need to throw up our hands and grab on to the hand of the One Who never changes, Who never fails, and Who is always with us.

Prayer

Father,
Thank you that you are more than we could ever ask or think. Thank you for the Holy Spirit and the resurrection power in us.

In Jesus' Name,
Amen!

51
Keep On!

Jesus told his disciples a parable
to show them they should
keep on praying and never give up.
Luke 18:1

What do you do when you've prayed and prayed and it seems nothing has changed, when the news gets worse and worse, and you wonder why you even bother?

You keep on praying; you keep on believing God! There is never a time when we should ever even contemplate giving up in prayer for a miracle.

In the book of Acts, God's people prayed, and people were healed, prison bars burst open, and lives were changed for eternity. They didn't have it easy, those folks! They were in danger of their very lives, but they kept on praying and believing God.

I talked to someone today who said, "God knows my heart, and I know He could just step in and take care of this, why doesn't He?" I wish I knew, I really do, but it's not our business to know why. It's our business to keep praying and trusting, ESPECIALLY when we don't understand why.

Here's a thought, when things look their worst, that's the time for us to hunker down and pray fervently, pray with passion, pray with singleness of mind and heart, pray as though our lives depended on it. There is power in prayer! God hears every cry of our hearts! Heaven takes notice when we pray! Pray on until the answer comes!

Prayer

Father,

Help me to keep on praying until I receive an answer.

Help me to trust you even if the answer isn't what I'm expecting. I know you do all things well.

In Jesus' Name,

Amen!

Notes

52
Uncertainty

Fear not, for I am with you;
Be not dismayed, for I am your God;
I will strengthen you.
I will help you,
I will uphold you with my righteous right hand.
Isaiah 41:10

I've mentioned before: Life! Is! Hard! This has been a week fraught with terrible news. One of my best friends in this world has been diagnosed with cancer. In the weeks prior to the diagnosis, our church family prayed for a miracle and for grace and mercy to surround this dear one and her family.

The miracle in the middle of a living nightmare is this: God is there, breathing peace, pouring grace, anointing with power, and reminding us even in the worst of times, He is Good! I can promise you one thing, in the midnight of our lives, God's goodness is evident. He can't be anything but good. I have seen God draw our church family together into a unity that is undeniably beautiful. We are leaning hard on God for this woman we all love beyond words. She and her family assure us they can feel the prayers.

As if that wasn't enough to keep us on our knees, this morning I picked up my phone to check my messages and as I read the first one, my heart nearly stopped, and my spirit recoiled. A beautiful woman who was a powerhouse in the Kingdom passed away. My mind couldn't take it in. I didn't even know she was sick. She didn't broadcast it, just trusted God all along the way to carry her over the uncertain road on which she traveled. Today she is rejoicing in the presence of the King.

The human in us cries out, "Why, Lord! She was vibrant, she was an encouragement, she invested in the lives of others!" And the answer fills our souls; "You don't need to understand, just trust me." And I do trust Him. With all my heart. It occurred to me this morning that we are reeling from the passing of this beautiful soul and yet when she breathed her last this side of eternity, she stepped into the welcoming arms of Jesus! Now that's something to rejoice about! And so, through our tears and heartache we thank God she is free at last. Isn't that what we all are working toward? After all, when we gave our hearts to Jesus, that was one of the big perks, am I right? Heaven with Jesus for all eternity!

Life is full of uncertainty. The phone can ring, and our lives are changed forever. I am encouraged by these words from II Corinthians 4:17 - For our present troubles are small and won't last very long. Yet they produce for us a glory that vastly outweighs them and will last forever!

Yes, life is difficult. We will grieve the rest of our lives because of the empty chair at the table, the absence of their dear voices, the birthday card we can't buy for the child who has gone ahead of us; but it wasn't meant to last forever. One day we will say goodbye to this world and step into our real home! The one that Jesus himself is preparing for us. We will be reunited with our friends and loved ones. We will say goodbye to pain, sickness, and death, but most of all we will see Jesus and it will be worth it all! We will have all of eternity together!

Prayer

Father, Thank You for the promise that this life is not all there is. Help me to remember that when faced with troubles of various kinds. In Jesus' Name, Amen!

53

Faith over Fear

I sought the Lord, and He answered me
and delivered me from all my fears.
Psalm 34:4

Can we talk about waiting again? To say it's hard is a gross understatement. It can be downright debilitating. We can become so consumed with the thing we are waiting for that we can barely function! You've been there, right? Or you might even be there now.

The thing is while you're waiting and praying and hoping, the devil is trying his hardest to send you to the farthest reaches of the land of what if! Am I right? What if I can't make the car payment this month? What if I don't get that raise? What if my doctor's report comes back and it's not good? Oh, that's one he loves to play with.

I was talking to someone one day and she was so terrified while waiting on the results of her mammogram that she thought about what she would wear on their head when she lost her hair from chemo. The devil had her convinced the report would be, well, not good! It turns out she got a good report. Praise God! But during her time of waiting the devil tormented her until she was consumed with negative, distorted thoughts.

Paul urges us in Philippians 4:6-7: Do not be anxious about anything, but in every situation, by prayer and petition, with thanksgiving, present your requests to God. And the peace of God, which transcends all understanding, will guard your hearts and your minds in Christ Jesus. I love, "will guard your hearts!" God's peace will shield, fortify, defend, and protect our hearts from Satan's darts, his hateful lies, and his sleazy deception. There is a stipulation here: we must pray about anything and everything, and we are to thank God as we pray that we know He is working on our behalf. His peace is available to all of us. Reach out today and take it!

Prayer

Father,

I am so ashamed that I sometimes allow fear to trick me into doubting You. Please forgive me and give me strength and grace to overcome fear with faith.

In Jesus Name,

Amen

54
He Loves Me

For God so loved the world that He gave
His only begotten Son
that whosoever believes in Him
will not perish but have everlasting life.
John 3:16

I read this recently: "I may not be perfect, but Jesus thinks I'm to die for!" Tears filled my eyes as I thought about that wonderful truth. I will never get over the wonder that Jesus WILLINGLY laid down His life for me.

How marvelous, how perfectly amazing, how enthralling, that the precious, perfect, Prince of Heaven stepped down from Paradise to suffer, bleed and die for me.

He is absolutely irresistible, and I can't get enough of Him. He is my everything. He is my first thought in the morning and my last thought before sleep overtakes me. I am completely and utterly in love with Him and HIs WORD. And today I'm more thankful than ever that death could not stop Him, the grave could not hold Him, and "because He lives, life is worth the living!" Thank you, Bill Gaither, for that song

His grace is amazing, His love is overwhelming, His mercy is never ending. He brought me through the fire, lifted me out of the pit, and provided everything I needed along the way.

He is available. He never sleeps or slumbers. His eye is on us, and His ear is open to our call. The very one who created you loves you more than you can begin to imagine. He is there in the good times, celebrating with you. He is there in the hard times, His tears mingling with Yours. He never gets tired of you asking for help. Everything we tell Him is of the utmost importance to Him. He gets you when other people are trying to figure you out. He is crazy about you!

If you don't know Him, you are missing out on LIVING LIFE TO THE FULLEST (thank you, Jason Roe). If you don't know Him already, I invite you to come to Him. You won't be disappointed!

Prayer

Father,

I worship You for Who you are even though my mind is so in awe. I am humbled that you love me with all my foibles. I can't imagine living my life without you.
In Jesus' Name, Amen!

55
Submission

He went on a little farther
and bowed with His face to the ground,
praying, My Father! If it is possible,
let this cup of suffering be taken away from me.
Yet I want your will to be done, not mine.
Matthew 26:39

During my quiet time one morning, it occurred to me (ok, sometimes I'm a little slow) that Jesus knew from the beginning of time His life would be the ultimate sacrifice for our sin.

Jesus was one hundred percent God and one hundred percent human. (I'm not good at math, but even I know that is nothing short of miraculous.)

Here's the thing, the God in Jesus knew what He would face. He knew about the scourging, the mocking, the spitting, the slapping, the sword in his side, and the nails in His hands and feet. He knew it and the human in Him dreaded it with the very fiber of His being. We know this because He prayed He wouldn't have to do it. He prayed until His sweat became like drops of blood. But here's the clincher: He prayed, "I dread this with everything in me. Please get me out of this, BUT.I want Your will to be done, not mine".

Now, I know that was hard because I have had to pray that same prayer. Somehow, though, knowing Jesus chose to surrender to the will of God, makes it easier for me to relinquish my will into the Father's hands. Jesus suffered unimaginable torture but look how it turned out! In the end, He arose the Victor over sin, death, hell, and the grave! And because He chose the Father's will over His own, we are reaping eternal benefits. Be encouraged, submitting to the will of God isn't always the easiest thing to do, but it's always the best!

Prayer

Father,

We want life to be perfect without any trials, but the truth is, life is hard. Help me to continually yield to your perfect plan for my life knowing you are with me every step of the way and that you will bring good from everything I experience.

In Jesus' conquering Name.

Amen!

56
He Is Here

The LORD your God
is in your midst—a warrior bringing victory.
He will create calm with his love;
He will rejoice over you with singing.
Zephaniah 3:17

He's in our midst! He isn't standing far off; He isn't looking DOWN from heaven! He is right here, right smack dab in the middle of us. He is all up in what we are going through.

He cares enough to take special notice of us exactly when we need Him. And you know what? He's not just there......He. Is. Mighty! Oh, and He isn't just mighty, He is ALL mighty! He is impressively powerful!

What does that mean for you and me? Child of God, it means He's in control! He is not just aware of what we are facing, He is going to do something about it. It's not our business to know the how, the why or the when. And in the meantime, "He will create calm with His love."

It is possible to go into the fiercest battle, to brave the most intense storm, to overcome the greatest obstacle and have peace that amazes and astounds us.

I mean, the natural reaction to devasting circumstances is fear, anxiety, and doubt. Oh, but when He is in the midst, everything changes. Today, whatever you are experiencing, God is right there with you right in the middle of it all. Trust and rest in the assurance of His presence.

Prayer

Father, You know me so well. You know how fearful life can be. Thank you for the promise of your presence right where I am. In Jesus' Mighty Name, Amen!

Notes

57
Storms

Then He arose and rebuked the wind,
and said to the sea, "Peace, be still!"
And the wind ceased and there was a great calm.

Mark 4:39

It's been said, "Into a life, a little rain must fall." I call that an understatement if there ever was one. The fact is, sometimes storms of epic proportions threaten to destroy us.

As flood waters from Hurricane Harvey rose across Houston and other areas of Texas, people found themselves trapped. But all was not lost as people banded together and formed human chains to rescue them from the murky waters that continued to rise all around them.

The disciples understood what being in a storm was all about. They found themselves on the Sea of Galilee being battered by a storm and nearly drowned by the waves. They were terrified, and they woke Jesus. "Hey, I know you're tired, but we are dying here." (My version) Jesus got up and said, "Be still." Immediately the storm obeyed. The disciples were amazed that even the wind and sea deferred to Him. When Jesus speaks, all nature comes to attention.

It occurs to me that there are people all around us who are experiencing life threatening storms. They are trapped by disease, financial crunches, by relational issues which bring doubt, confusion, and fear. They feel alone in their struggle to survive! Beloved, that's when the Family of God forms a chain that reaches to the throne of God. It is there we intercede for those who may be in such exhaustion and distress they can't pray for themselves. What an honor it is to lay these precious ones at the feet of the One Who is able! As we pray fervently and believe steadfastly, those whom the storm has afflicted, will hear the voice of Jesus say, "Be still." Oh, what victory they will experience! They made it through!

God hasn't promised we won't have storms, but He has promised to provide exactly what we need when we need it as we wait for the calm that follows the storm.

For those of you going through your own personal storm today, take heart; the storm won't last forever. The promise of Sonlight is just ahead.

Prayer

Father,

There are those who are experiencing the storm of their lives. Please bring your assurance, peace, and comfort to sustain them as they traverse the waves. May they be encouraged by the prayers of the saints of God as they are lifted continually before the mercy seat.

In the mighty name of Jesus, Amen!

58
The Answer

Let us then with confidence draw near
to the throne of grace, that we may receive mercy
and find grace to help in time of need.
Hebrews 4:16

Did you take time this morning to spend time with your Heavenly Father? If not, do you have plans to make time during the day to forget about everything else, sit down, and delight in being with the One who loves you most?

As I travel to churches to preach or to retreats to share, one thing becomes plain. We need to spend time in communion with God. People are discouraged, they are disillusioned, they are disappointed in people and in circumstances. They need answers. I don't have them. As people share their hearts with me, I want so much to fix the brokenness I find there. The truth is, I can't! What I CAN do is point them to the One who doesn't just have the answers, He IS the answer!

It occurs to me that God doesn't always take us out of our circumstances. He doesn't always make a way around an obstacle in our path. But He will take us THROUGH the most difficult of circumstances and provide the strength we need to get OVER the obstacle.

All the while He cheers us on with His abiding presence, He provides grace and strength and comfort, so we can keep going as we traverse a rough, rocky road!

I encourage you today to steal away somewhere with Jesus. Take time to bless His sweet heart by laying everything else aside and coming to Him for refreshment. There you will find a heart that understands your deepest longings. It will be the best part of your day.

Prayer

Father,

　　Help me to understand how important it is to spend time in your presence. I need grace to get through each day. Help me to set aside a special time daily to talk to you.

In Jesus' Name, Amen!

Notes

59
Overcoming Grace

You planned evil against me; God planned it for good.
Genesis 50:20

I've been thinking about Joseph. The Old Testament Joseph. The Coat of Many Colors Joseph.

When I was a little girl, the story of Joseph's coat was one of my favorites. As I've grown older and really gotten into the meat of the WORD, I've come to realize there is so much more to Joseph than a pretty coat.

In the early accounts of Joseph and his brothers, Joseph seems to be a tattletale and a braggart. Maybe we can just chalk all that up to his immaturity, but I can see why his brothers didn't like him much. Ok, they hated his guts. (My mother just turned over in her grave.)

Joseph's brothers have had enough, and they sell him to some Ishmaelites, who in turn sell him to a rich Egyptian named Potiphar. The Bible tells us, "The LORD was with Joseph so that he prospered, and when his master saw that the LORD was with him and that the LORD gave him success in everything he did, he put Joseph in charge of his household."

Isn't that just like our God to bless us and cause us to prosper even when it seems the devil is having his way with us? Read on. Now Potiphar's wife, well let's just say she had designs on Joseph. Joseph is a gentleman, maybe that particular grace was inspired by his mother, Rachel. Who knows?

What we do know is that Joseph repeatedly refused to fall into the trap laid by this rich, bored, Egyptian housewife. That malicious, malevolent monster accused him of rape and

Potiphar, who fell for it hook, line, and sinker had Joseph put in prison. Again, the Bible tells us, while Joseph was there in the prison, "The LORD was with him, and He showed him kindness and granted him favor in the eyes of the prison warden."

The warden put Joseph in charge of all those held in the prison, and he was made responsible for all that was done there. The warden paid no attention to anything under Joseph's care, because "the LORD was with Joseph and gave him success in whatever he did." I think we can see God's hand in this.

Joseph interprets the dream of the King's cup bearer, who was also unfortunately incarcerated, asking only to be remembered to the King when the cup bearer is finally freed. The cup bearer apparently got amnesia when he returned to court, and Joseph continues his jail time. Ah, but God!

The King has a vison no one can interpret and suddenly, the cup bearer comes out of his daze and remembers Joseph. Joseph is sent for and not only tells the King the meaning of the dreams, which foretells a great famine, but he has the solution. The King makes him governor over Egypt, second only to the King.

Now looking at it from here, that is a very long way from a pit in Dothan. I guess you could say Joseph went from the pit to the pinnacle.

It certainly took Joseph a long time to get to God's plan for his life. Or did it? I think God engineered every bit of the journey to the fulfilment of that plan. To get to where he was going, Joseph had to endure hatred, hardship, and heartlessness. But he persisted and he prevailed.

While we've never been thrown in a pit because our siblings were jealous of us, or accused unjustly and put into prison, I would venture to say we have all been prisoners of our circumstances and we have all had to endure adversity.

Looking back, we can see God's hand was on us and His Spirit guided us as we traversed unfamiliar and somewhat dangerous territory.

Like Joseph, we are His favored ones, not just favored but HIGHLY favored! He delights in us. He plans for us, and He has promised to never leave or forsake us. Not ever, not once, under no circumstances, by no means! His presence is not just for the good times, but for all the times of our lives.

Prayer

Father,

When I'm tempted to feel sorry for myself, let me remember Joseph and the overcoming grace you provided for him. That grace is sufficient for me!

Thank you!

In Jesus' Name, Amen!

Notes

60
When God Says "No"

For the Lord God is a sun and shield,
the Lord gives grace and glory;
no good thing does He withhold
from those who walk uprightly
Psalm 84:11

I'm a pray-er. I believe in prayer. I believe in the power of prayer. I believe God answers prayer.

Having said all that, I confess I sometimes don't know how to pray. I remember when our son Jason was sick and given less than a year to live, I prayed with all my heart that he would be healed so that he could raise his children, see them marry and have children. I claimed verse after verse of scripture. I cried, I pleaded, I begged.

Jason was not healed this side of eternity. He passed from this world into the next on July 13, 2012. I know he is perfect and whole, happy, and free, but sometimes, I've felt as though believing that was a cop out.

Let me explain. I was not shy about telling anyone and everyone I believed my child would be healed. I was convinced. I didn't doubt it. It was not a faith issue. My faith was strong and sure. Someone asked me how it was working out for me since I believed but didn't get what I believed for. Can I say, I wanted to smack them? It wasn't working out. I was struggling. I was hurting. I was disappointed in God's decision to take my son. And I didn't know if I could ever again pray for someone to be healed. If my faith wasn't enough to heal my precious child, I knew I couldn't summon enough to pray for someone else. I was in a dark and confusing place.

My children and my husband felt the same way. However, somewhere along the way, the Spirit of God led me to a scripture that sealed the deal for me. "Now this is the confidence that we have in Him, that if we ask anything ACCORDING to His WILL, He hears us" (1 John 11:14).

It wasn't God's will to heal Jason. Plain and simple! Hard to swallow, but there it was! I chewed on that verse for a few days and realized my struggle was in surrendering to the will of God. A deep and profound peace filled my broken heart and spirit. It wasn't that those of us who prayed didn't have powerful faith or that the prayers that bombarded the throne weren't fervent enough. It wasn't because we did anything wrong. It was not in God's plan. Somehow, that knowledge comforted me.

Do I understand why it wasn't in the great design of our Creator to banish Jason's cancer to the pit of hell where it belonged? No and I may never. But this one thing I do know. I don't have to understand God. I just have to trust Him. Oh, and I do! I know in His sovereignty; He always knows what's best. He loves me and even if I don't understand Him, He totally gets me! And that is enough.

Today, I am able to pray for healing for others. I know that God can heal! I know He still does heal! Whatever happens, we can trust Him!

Prayer

Father,

It's hard when Your answer to our fervent prayers is not what we had hoped for. But I thank you for never making a mistake. I can trust you even when I don't' understand.

In Jesus' Name,
Amen!

61
Passing the Test

And God tested Abraham.

Genesis 22:1

And what a test it was! God didn't ASK Abraham, He COMMANDED Abraham to take his only son Isaac and sacrifice him on an altar. I have to pause and take a deep breath after thinking about that.

Let me lay it out for you. God had promised Abraham he would have a son. He made it clear that Isaac was the heir of the promise. God had promised He would give Abraham more descendants than could be numbered and those descendants would come through Isaac. And now God has told Abraham to take Isaac and sacrifice him on an altar.

I can't wait to get to heaven and ask Abraham how the journey of three days to Moriah went. Imagine with me. Abraham knows he has three days with his precious son. I know I would have been tense, tearful, and terrified about what was to take place. I would have hugged my child so many times, he would have begged me to stop. I would not have let him out of my sight. I would have memorized everything he said and did. I would have stamped his image on my heart. And at night when everyone settled down to sleep, I would have cried until exhaustion overcame me and I fell into a fitful sleep only to awaken to the dawn of the cruel reality. I'm sure it happened just that way.

Then comes the question Abraham has been dreading. "Father, we have wood, and we have fire, but where is the lamb?"

Swallowing the bile that has risen in his throat, commanding the tears not to streak his face, and taking a deep breath, Abraham stalwartly replies, "God will supply a lamb."

131

You know it occurs to me that Abraham believed God's provision would bestow a lamb for the offering or, if not, He would give Abraham the courage, grace, and strength to obey. And so, on they went.

When they arrive at Moriah, Abraham puts wood on the altar and begins to bind Isaac. Don't you know by this time, Isaac has figured out what is going on? My imagination runs wild as I envision this boy begging his father to have mercy. But Abraham doggedly proceeds. He places Isaac on the altar, raises his knife, but wait! God calls out to Abraham, "Don't touch the boy!" Abraham realizes God has indeed provided a ram. One is caught in the bushes.

How do you spell relief? Even as I write, I heave a huge sigh! That was a close call, wasn't it? The moral of the story is this. God didn't test Abraham to see what Abraham would do, in his omniscience, He already knew. The test was so Abraham could see what God would do. Think about that! And God was faithful and right on time. The next time you are put to the test, instead of worrying over what you're going to do, trust and obey and watch to see what your mighty, miraculous, merciful Father will do! You won't be disappointed.

Prayer

Father,

As I ponder the story of Abraham and Isaac, my heart is filled with the knowledge that you are our provider. Help me to trust you and to be obedient no matter what you ask of me.

In Jesus' Name,
Amen!

62
Surviving the Drought

I will be as the dew...
Hosea 14:5

There is nothing so beautiful as the early hours of the morning when dawn breaks. I love this time of the day. The air is still and cool and pure. The cacophony of nature serenades with music almost too sweet for human ears. And the dew, the refreshing, thirst quenching dew covers the ground.

God told Hosea He would be as dew to Israel and cause them to blossom and their roots to go deep.

Do you ever feel parched, so dry in fact that it's as though you could crumble if someone looked at you the wrong way? You are weak, devoid of power, you're worn out, and worn down. We've all been there. But don't despair. God has promised to send the dew of His presence to revive us from our dried-up existence. Can you picture it? The presence of God settling on us like dew on scorched ground. Dew that will satisfy and sustain us through the winds of persecution, discouragement and frustration that blow hot.

Oh, but there's more! He said he would make us blossom. What a promise! Do you catch it? He's not just going to refresh us; He will make us bloom! Instead of our souls being shriveled up like a prune, we will bloom with the joy of the Lord. And when we bloom others will see the miracle that has taken place in us. We will be a beacon of hope to those who thirst for a drink of water that never runs dry.

And He's still not finished, He will cause our roots to go deep, so that even in the fiercest gale we will not be moved! What a blessed afterward! We survived the drought, we have been refreshed, refilled, and rooted deep in the promises and power of God, our Father!

133

Prayer

Father,

What a blessing, what a promise! Thank you for the dew of your presence to the arid soil of my heart. You are always what I need.

In Jesus' Name,

Amen!

63
The God Who Sees

She gave this name to the LORD who spoke to her:
"You are the God who sees me,"
for she said, "I have now seen the One who sees me.
Genesis 16:13

I love the story of Abraham and Sarah. God promised them a son when they were well past childbearing age. Sarah laughed, because she thought it was an utter impossibility. She was so sure she wouldn't have a child that she gave her servant, Hagar, to Abraham.

Hagar became pregnant and then the sparks began to fly. Sarah was jealous, Hagar was disdainful. She was pregnant with the master's child. Surely that gave her some leverage. You would think but wait. Sarah complained to Abraham, and he said, "Do whatever you want with her." (Just like a man to pass the buck. Bless his heart!) So, Sarah sent her away. Poor Hagar, given to her master for breeding purposes, run off by a jealous wife, and now alone and afraid in the wilderness.

I'm sure none of us have had that exact experience, but we have all had moments in our lives when we felt frightened and forgotten. But let's look further, an angel sent from the throne room of God came to Hagar, right where she was, in the wasteland of her precarious position. He reassured her that God knew right where she was and despite her circumstances, she would have a son, his name would be Ishmael and he would birth a great nation. I'm sure she perked up right away. She called the name of that place, "The God Who Sees." I love it! Don't you?

Do you catch the significance? No matter where we are, no matter who has made us feel unworthy. No matter if we have been taken advantage of, abused, or neglected. No matter if we've been dumped by our spouse, or duped by our friend, we serve a God who sees. And he is keeping score.

I'm sure Hagar returned to Sarah with a new determination to keep on keeping on. Why? Because God had seen her at her lowest point, and He had given her hope.

Today, wherever you are in your life, there is always hope. There is always a way out because we are in relationship with a God who sees. And He sees you in your wilderness, wherever that may be. Look up! Help is on the way!

Prayer

Father,
I'm so glad you see me.

I'm thankful I am important to you. Help me to remember that when it seems things are falling apart. Help me also know you will provide what I need right where I am.

In Jesus' Name,
Amen!

64
Pig in the House

Look not on his countenance,
or on the height of his stature;
because I have refused him:
for the Lord sees not as man sees;
for man looks on the outward appearance,
but the Lord looks on the heart.
1 Samuel 16:7

Our daughter and her family live in a beautiful home in a beautiful neighborhood. To visit them is a delight to the senses. They are a lovely family made up of two parents, three kids, a dog, six cats and a pig. Yes, I said "pig". His name is Oliver Todd Quigley, and he is a much-loved member of the family. He is house broken. He actually squeals when he has to go out and are you ready? He does tricks!!! Personally, I'm attached to him. I think he is the sweetest little piggy wiggy ever.

I was recently talking to one of my family members about him going out to potty. She asked, (what many people probably are thinking), "Doesn't he want to roll in the mud when he goes outside?" I laughed. "No, he doesn't," I replied, "he is cleaner than the dog." It's true. I've taken him out a few times and not once has he even tried to roll on the ground. He doesn't smell either. When you walk in the house, if you didn't know a pig lived there you would never suspect. The truth is pigs have a bad reputation. If they are raised in the mud, they will roll in the mud, but if you clean them up, give them a clean place to live, they are model pets.

It reminds me of how we are with some people. Perhaps we have heard about some of the things they did before they found Jesus. "Did you know she ran around on her husband

137

before she got saved? I hope she really got saved, but I'll have to see it to believe it." Or "He had a gambling addiction; I hope he still doesn't have that nasty habit."

Maybe we have formed opinions about them based on what we have heard from others, and we become biased and unwilling to give them a chance. We determine in our little judgmental hearts we will keep them at arm's length.

It's a good thing Jesus didn't care about what people were before they were in relationship with Him. Instead, He saw what they could become. If Jesus had paid attention to how people felt about Matthew, He would have walked right on by. Instead, He said, "Follow me!" Matthew did! He made restitution! He was a changed man! Oh, and Peter! He was a big mouth braggart who denied Jesus three times. Jesus knew that would happen when He called Peter, but he gave Peter a chance. Peter repented, sold out, and became a driving force in the early church.

What about you and me? We may not have committed any of the "big" sins (I'm shaking my head), but we were headed for a place called hell until Jesus saw something in us that was worth saving. See, it doesn't matter who you WERE, it's who you ARE. And if you are saved, no matter what your past issues, you belong to Jesus. He has chosen to forget your sin. Now as someone who has experienced transformation, shouldn't we be looking at others with the mind of Christ and through His eyes?

Prayer

Father, When I am tempted to judge others, help me remember where I was and who I was before you found me. Forgive me for the times I have judged others. Let me see them through your eyes. In Jesus' Name, Amen!

65
It Is Well!

Did you ever feel as if you had an appointment with God? That's exactly how I felt one morning here in the beauty of South Carolina. We are so blessed to enjoy the majestic mountain vistas in Wild Wonderful West Virginia on a daily basis. God is an awesome artist! However, this bit of blessing came right smack dab in the middle of some of the coldest weather we have experienced in our six years in the Mountain State.

As I picked up my Bible to begin my quiet time, my eyes fell on this passage, "Say to the righteous, that it shall be well with them" (Isaiah 3:10).

My heart nearly overflowed with blessing! It shall be well. What a promise to those who are traversing rocky, seemingly endless terrain! What a piece of assurance to those who are enjoying the mountain top, with the Son shining brightly on them and the work to which they have been called. What a statement of solid promise from the One who loves us! Here come the tears! Our God is good! He is good when things are going as planned, He is good when our plans fail on every level. He is good when we are healthy, He is good when we aren't! He. Is. Good. It's Who He is. He can't be anything but good.

I was talking with a precious friend the other day. We talked about some of the darkest places we have been through. We reminisced about the times we had had the very same discussion and we wondered, How can anything good come from the sorrow we have experienced?" The truth is we may never know this side of heaven, but we have the promise from our Father that "it shall be well".

Oh, child of God, please let those words sink deep into your inmost being. It. Shall. Be. Well! No matter what happens, His grace, His mercy, His comfort, His sustaining power are there with us to take us through places we would never venture by ourselves. Take heart today! It shall be well!

Prayer

Father,
Help me to remember that it is always well when I trust you.
    In Jesus' Name,
    Amen!

66
Did God Really Say…?

When he lies, he speaks his native language,
for he is a liar
and the father of lies.
John 8:34

Adam and Eve are like the relatives you really aren't sure you want people to know about. They had it so good, didn't they? A beautiful, tropical paradise where everything they needed was supplied; trees to shade them from the heat of the day, and beautiful rivers in which to swim and bathe, a supply of nutritious, delicious food to eat. They even had authority over the animals in the beautiful garden. Think about it: They could hold baby lions and tigers and pet those little babies' mamas and daddies. But most of all, they were in relationship with God Himself. They walked with Him and had conversations with Him in the cool of the day. What more could they want? Well, Satan made sure there was more to be had. And they blew it!

More is not always better, (you know that when you get on the scales the next day after you have had three pieces of death by chocolate cake) but he made it look so enticing. In essence he told them, "God is just being selfish, He knows if you eat the fruit from the forbidden tree, you will be just as smart as He is, and He certainly doesn't want that." OOOOH, that old liar was so smug, and he made Eve doubt God and His love, so she gave in, and she coaxed Adam into doing the same.

We look down on Adam and Eve because they are the reason we have all the problems we have. But think on this. We get in trouble most of the time because we want to be as smart as God. That sounds familiar, doesn't it? We sometimes think we know what is good for us. We let the devil convince

141

us that we ARE smarter than God and that we need to help our Heavenly Father with our problem.

We begin by allowing the devil to make us doubt God and His love. We allow him to make us wonder if God really cares, and the door to our hearts opens just a smidgen. He gives it a little shove and strolls in for a visit. And that's all she wrote! It's never good when we allow ourselves to converse with the devil.

Yes, I got all that from a few verses in Genesis. That's a great storyline, but it's not there just so you will be able to read about an exciting adventure which will amaze and astound you. God inspired Moses to write about Adam and Eve because He hoped we would learn from their mistakes. Sadly, most of us have to fail before we really learn the lesson. God means what He says and says what He means. Do not eat, means "not even a nibble." Think on that the next time you're tempted to ignore "thou shalt not…"

Prayer

Father,

Help me to recognize the voice of the enemy when he comes at me with his lying tongue. Help me to submit myself to You and to resist him, and when I do, He has to run.

In Jesus' Name,

Amen!

67
Continue Steadfastly

And now, Lord, look upon their threats
and grant to your servants
to continue to speak your word with all boldness.
Acts. 4:29

After the day of Pentecost, the church grew from a little body of 120 believers to a Mega Church of 3,000! Scripture tells us the people "continued steadfastly." I love that.

This early church didn't have it easy. They were persecuted, pursued, and pestered. But the Bible says, they "continued steadfastly." These folks were convinced Jesus was real and they were resolute in their commitment to His cause. They didn't quit or go into hiding when the going got tough, they just kept on praying and "continued steadfastly."

When Peter and John were put in prison because they healed a lame man and then told not to preach Jesus, they told their persecutors, "Seriously? We are going to obey God even if you don't like it!" (my translation). When they were released, they didn't disappear into obscurity, they went to a prayer meeting and prayed for boldness to continue preaching the Good News of Jesus.

How often, when we are faced with a difficult set of circumstances, are we inclined to run and hide? It's natural, I suppose, but for the Child of God it isn't an option. There is a whole world out there waiting to see how we act and react when we face challenges that threaten our well-being. We don't have any other choice but to "continue steadfastly." God has promised to provide what we need during those times of testing! Not only that, but He also promised to be with us through the trial. What part of "I'll never leave you or forsake you," don't we understand?

Beloved, hold on, hold still, hold tight, your God is for you. He will walk with you through the fire of fierce opposition, and He will bring you through! Hallelujah!

Prayer

Father,

Your word says the Holy Spirit will give us power to witness. Fill me with fresh anointing each day that I will be bold and fearless in my quest to tell others about the saving grace of Jesus.

In His Name,
Amen!

68
I Can Do It!

I don't know about you, but I get a little overwhelmed sometimes with all I have to do. I become physically tired, and you know how the devil loves to kick us when we're down. I'm glad I learned, early on, the importance of quiet time with God before I face my day.

One morning I was reading Psalm 138 and verse eight planted itself deep in my heart. The LORD will perfect that which concerns me! Just a simple sentence, but fraught with truth. Potent!

Perfect (the verb) means finish, achieve, reach the summit, refine, sharpen. I love words and I especially love those words. As I chewed on them, swallowed, and digested the significance of that promise for me today, verse eight infused me with hope. I can finish the things I have to do; I can achieve the goals I have set for myself; I can reach the summit of promise and potential. All the while, the Holy Spirit is refining me and making me a sharp instrument so I can be used of God more effectively.

Child of God, are you crushed by the weight of your circumstances? Are you inundated with responsibilities and duties? Are you living in defeat, humiliation, and mortification? Have you allowed yourself to be royally trounced by the devil? I say "allowed" because we don't have to take that mess he tries to throw our way. We have power over his very power! Don't believe me? Then believe the words of Jesus from Luke 10:19, "Behold, I have given you authority to tread on serpents and scorpions, and over all the power of the enemy, and nothing shall hurt you."

There it is! Read it. Believe it. Live it! He will perfect that which concerns you! That is a certainty in a world where not much else is.

Prayer

Father,

Help me to remember your words. You will help me achieve the plans you have for me and even my own plans in accordance with your will. I don't need to be frustrated, or overwhelmed, as I am submissive to your Holy Spirit.

In Jesus' Name,

Amen!

69
God Is With Us

Behold, the virgin shall conceive and bear a son, and they
shall call His name Immanuel
which means, God with us.
Matthew 1:22-23

God is involved in my life and has been since my beginning, I mean my VERY beginning. Psalm 139 tells us He saw us when we were being formed and He watched us grow in our mother's womb. He was there the day we first saw the light of day, when the doctor smacked our bottom, and when we first looked in the eyes of our mother. He already had a plan in place for us.

There was a baby boy who was born four years before I was. God already knew that little boy would grow up to be my husband. I giggle in wonder at the magnificence of God's planning for me.

He knows us intimately. In other words, He knows what makes us tick. He wants us to know Him in all his fullness. He wants us to trust His heart, hold His hand and follow His leading. I'm listening to Christmas music again (don't judge me). Immanuel, God WITH us! What a powerful truth.

Until the birth of Jesus, God spoke to men and women through prophets. But Jesus came right straight to where we were and became like us to experience earthly, human, day to day, nitty gritty living. He came to be WITH us because He loved us so much.

When He went back home to heaven, He sent His Holy Spirit to live IN us so we could know the meaning of God WITH us every second of every day. We are never alone. He never takes His eyes off of us. He never stops interceding for us. The bottom line is this, Jesus is available to us, any time, and any place. You only have to breathe His name. You can know Him as fully as you want to. The choice is yours!

Prayer

Father,

Thank you for the promise of your presence. I am enthralled by the truth that you are WITH me. Help me to never take it for granted, but to celebrate You every day of my life.

In Jesus' Name,

Amen!

70
I Want to Love You More

The eternal God is your dwelling place,
and underneath are the everlasting arms….
Deuteronomy 33:2

"Lord, I want to love you more," I prayed one day. "Help me to love you more." I hesitated to voice my thoughts (even though I know God already knew them).

As a born-again child of God, shouldn't I automatically love God supremely? I did love Him. I had loved him almost my whole life. And yet, I knew I didn't love Him enough. I loved Him because He saved me. I loved him because He was good and usually, I got everything I prayed for. I loved him because He was there for me when I needed a shoulder. Still, something missing. I wanted to be madly in love with Him. I wanted Him to be my first thought in the morning and my last at night. I wanted to wake up in the middle of the night and think about Him. I wanted to love Him not just for what He did, but I wanted to love Him for WHO is was and is.

My mama used to warn me, "Be careful what you ask for, make sure it's what you really want because you just might get it." Little did I know when God answered my prayer, He would take me on a journey I never expected, and He would show me things I really never wanted to see. In His wisdom, He knew I needed some experiences to teach me to love Him more.

How was I to know the death of my sweet son Jason would show me the goodness of God in unimaginable ways, would teach me lessons I didn't know I needed to learn and would enable me to love God in a deeper, more unquestioning, unrestrained way?

The depths of grief to which I descended, taught me I didn't need anyone or anything but God, because nothing or no one could say or do anything to staunch the bleeding of my wounded spirit.

He loved me when I laid on the floor face down and tried to pray, but the only words I could speak were, "Oh, God!" Over and over. He loved me even when I told Him how disappointed I was in His decision not to heal my son this side of eternity. He just let me talk, He never scolded, or judged or punished me. He never left me when I found it hard to trust Him.

God didn't say much, He just held me until I was ready to listen. And when He spoke, the pieces of my broken heart began to respond to His healing words. It wasn't an easy journey. It was fraught with pain and sorrow and sometimes utter despair. I breathe deeply as I write these words.

As I began to emerge from my cocoon of grief, I was confronted with a deep truth. I loved God more than I ever had. I trusted Him more than I thought I ever could. I knew what it was to pass through the Valley of the Shadow of death and have my Father walk with me and to encourage me to keep on going.

The lessons I learned in the dark night of my soul might never have been learned had I walked an easy road. There have been other roads with ruts and obstacles and God has never failed me. With each adventure, my love for Him goes deeper, truer, stronger, and I find I can rely on Him to lead me even when I can't see where I'm going. He knows the way.....He IS the way!

Prayer

Father, You are such a loving, patient Father. Thank you for always being there to celebrate the good times and to hold me during the hard times. In Jesus' Name, Amen!

71

Put on your Armor

Put on the full armor of God,
so that you will be able to stand firm
against the schemes of the devil.
Ephesians 6:11

I urge you to stay alert and put your armor on. I don't want to burst your bubble, but I have an announcement. "THE DEVIL IS ALIVE AND WELL!" Most of you probably knew that already, having been embroiled in battle with him for a while, but the rest of you, open your eyes, keep your guard up, he is just waiting for an opportunity to infiltrate, steal, kill and destroy. He wants to infiltrate our churches, families and friendships and cause division, dissension, and deceit. He wants brothers and sisters in Christ to lose confidence in each other. He will cause them to be jealous of one another, and to hold grudges. He wants to steal the glory from Almighty God and cause our attention to be focused on things other than winning the lost at any cost.

He wants to kill relationships, ruin influences, and quench the spirit of God. He wants to destroy friendships, lives, and reputations. And if we aren't careful, he will be well on his way to success before we even realize he's got his hands all up in our business.

One of the things that will hurt us most is not recognizing the devil for who and what he is. We need to be ready to "nip it, nip it, nip it," as Barney Fife says on the Andy Griffith show. We can't allow the devil to have a toe hold. If he gets his foot in the door, the fight is on.

I urge you to keep your guard up. The devil will get in through a place where we least expect, and he will come at times when things are going well, and we feel invincible. He will be on us and have us in his clutches before we know what hit us.

The only way to win the battle is to fall on our knees before our Almighty God who is the Captain of the Army of the Host of Heaven. When we pray, God hears us, and He honors our prayers. He will go before us guiding us, keeping us, and cheering us on. And best of all, He will fight for us!

God intended for us to live in victory, not to wallow in defeat. Today, rise up! Have confidence in the God who is able, stand still and see the salvation of the Lord.

Prayer

Father,

Help me to put on your whole armor when I get up in the morning and help me to recognize my power as a spirit- filled child of God.

In Jesus' Name,
Amen!

72
Sing!

Enter His gates with thanksgiving;
Go into His courts with praise.
Give thanks to Him and praise His name.
Psalm 100:4

As I entered my quiet time with the Lord, it got, well, not so quiet. I started singing, "This is the day the Lord has made, let us rejoice and be glad in it." What a way to start the day! Of course, life has a way of trying to rob us of our joy. Traffic was ridiculous, and work was busy and demanding. I found myself becoming frustrated, then that same song came into my mind. I started singing again and the frustration and anxiety disappeared.

It's amazing what praising can do! It's an old cliché, but it is true! The Bible tells us in Psalm 22 that God inhabits the praises of His people. Yes, indeed He does! When we begin to sing and praise, heaven sits up and takes notice and God makes His presence known to us during some of the most exasperating moments of our lives. How can we stay annoyed and frustrated when we are in the presence of the King? We can't. Praise paves the way for miracles.

Remember Paul and Silas in the deep dark dungeon? They were in the nastiest of places. They were cold, hungry, and weary, but that didn't stop them from singing the praises of God at midnight. And God came in a big way to rescue them.

Oh, and my fave: King Jehoshaphat and Judah were about to be attacked by THREE armies. The King didn't waste any time in calling the people together for a prayer meeting. To make a long story short, when Jehoshaphat sent the army out, he appointed the choir to lead the march. And here's the best part of the story. As those Levites began to sing and praise,

The Lord sent an ambush. I'm shaking my head in wonder as I think about it once again. TWO of the armies fought against the THIRD army and destroyed them and the two armies that were left turned on each other. The Bible says, "They helped to destroy each other." And all the people of Judah had to do was pick up the spoils from the battles.

There is power in praise! The devil loves it when we sigh but he can't stand it when we sing! He won't stick around once the worship starts; I promise you!

Prayer

Father,

I praise you for all You do, but most of all I praise You for Who You are and who I am in You.

In Jesus' Name, Amen!

73
Who Told You?

For we are God's handiwork,
created in Christ Jesus to do good works,
which God prepared in advance for us to do.
Ephesians 2:10

I am thinking today of my mother; beautiful, funny, feminine, loving, and most of all godly. She once said to me, "What does God see in me, I have no talents, I'm not worthy of his call on my life?"

The fact is my mother was an amazing woman. My Daddy died when I wasn't quite eight. He was a pastor and had just overseen the building of a new church. After Daddy passed, the church voted for Mama to stay on as pastor. She was the quintessential pastor, and she had a way of loving people into the kingdom. If the devil tried to get a toehold, she stomped on that toe, and he went running.

As she loved the congregation, she took them deep into the Word and taught them about giving themselves completely to Jesus and living in victory. I'm here to tell you; the woman was and is a legend.

My mom had a childhood of abuse. Someone told her she was of no value except as an object of shame. Sadly, she was convinced. Those were the days when you kept quiet about what was happening at home, and she would have been mortified to know I was aware of her mistreatment. There were so many signs. One was her overprotection of me. I lived the most sheltered life imaginable. And I was never far from her sight or reach.

My mama would keep this secret, and for the rest of her life she lived with the shame of her childhood that hung like a chain around her neck. I find it sad that she never could escape the shackles that bound her. However, in spite of that, God used her in ways only eternity will tell.

I know there are those of you who suffer similarly. I want to ask you, Who told you that you weren't worthy, that you had no value, who said you were useless and just an object of shame? Who told you that you would never amount to anything, you would never be loved, and you would never get out of the hole you were buried neck deep in? WHO TOLD YOU?

I can assure you; it wasn't Jesus. And whoever told you was a liar. You know the Bible tells us the devil is a liar and the father of liars. When someone is lying to you, they are like the devil. Have you ever thought of that? All of us know the devil doesn't stick around to bring good into our lives. And honey, let me tell you, the enemy of your soul doesn't want you to go from striving to thriving. He wants to keep you in the muck and mire, in the cold, stinking ashes of despair, despondency, hopeless and helpless.

I have good news. Jesus came to set you free. And the Bible tells us, "Whom the Son sets free, is free indeed" (John 8:36). That means without a doubt, undeniably, really, certainly, definitely free. So today, I want you to think about who pushed you down in the ash filled pit in which you reside today? Think hard. Know these truths.

- You are the apple of God's eye (Zechariah 2:8).
- Your name is engraved on the palms of his hand
- (Isaiah 49:16).
- You are a royal priesthood, a holy nation (I Peter 2:9).
- You are a masterpiece (Ephesians 2:10 NLT).

Oh, I could go on and on. So today, who will you believe, the one who wants to keep you in the misery of the moment, or the One who loves you enough that He died for you? Can your mind comprehend that?

If He loved, you enough to die for you that tells me you are valued beyond price. Don't listen to the decades of lies the devil has poured into your spirit. Lift your face to the Son. Listen to what He has to tell you! And believe it with all your heart.

Prayer

Father,

Help me to always remember who I am in You. You have made me your child. You chose me. You saw something of worth in me.

Thank you!

In Jesus' Name, Amen!

74
And Beauty Keeps Rising!

To all who mourn in Israel,
He will give a crown of beauty for ashes,
a joyous blessing
instead of mourning,
festive praise instead of despair.
In their righteousness, they will be like great oak
s that the LORD has planted for His own glory.
Isaiah 61:3

Yesterday marked the tenth anniversary of our son Jason moving to heaven, his forever home. The enormity of it all pierced my heart. I confess I had a moment. Who of us, when confronted with an occasion such as this, isn't taken back to the very moment they learned they would never see their loved one again this side of heaven?

As the tears ran down my cheeks, my ever-present Heavenly Father began to remind me of Jason's reality. He was in heaven. He was with Jesus. He was free from sickness, pain, heartache, and sorrow. He wasn't troubled by politics, pollution, or problems. He was enjoying "his best life now." Jason reminded us over and over again, as he was preparing to move, "Live life to the fullest!" And here he is living the dream, only it isn't a dream! It's more real than what even we experience here on planet earth.

I began to thank the Lord that we knew Jason was dancing around the throne, and that we have a H O P E. Our hope is heaven and one day, we will once again hold sweet Jason in our arms and praise the Lord together that we made it through never to say good-bye again.

My tears turned to tears of joy! How could I be sorry that Jason was in such a beautiful, wonderful, glorious, place where there are no words to describe place! I could not, I would not,

159

and I was not! I am thankful we never have to be concerned about Jason again. He is ok. He is more than ok, and he always will be! God brought beauty from my ashes of grief and despair, and He keeps on bringing it! He is a God of generosity, of abundance, of extravagance. And He is pouring it out daily.

Those of you who shared my journey knew I had questions that were never answered, disappointment that God hadn't answered my prayers the way I thought He would, and fear my prayers hadn't been enough! Oh, dear heart, as I sat in the ashes, God showed me I didn't need to know the answers, I simply needed to trust Him. He never left me. He sat there with me, and He gave me the strength to rise from the ashes and reach for beauty.

You see, God can work ON you and even IN you while you're sitting in the ashes, but it's only when you rise up out of the ashes that He can work THROUGH you! The truth is, if there had been no ashes, there would have been no beauty. I would have continued along, not ever understanding the privilege of sitting in the ashes with Jesus. And my heart wouldn't have felt so connected to others who were sitting in ashes of their own. Because the fact is, until you've seen your hopes, dreams and prayers go up in smoke, you don't get it.

Not everyone has had to say good-bye to a child, but most of us have said good-bye to someone we love and as a result, we spent some time in the ashes. I know this: God is faithful, and if you will let Him, He'll bring you up and out. And not only that, but He will also make you a blessing beyond what you could ever imagined.

Prayer

Father, If I had never experienced the ashes, I would not have appreciated the beauty. Sometimes, lessons are hard, but they are needed and necessary. I know you understand and I'm thankful. In Jesus' Name, Amen!

75
We Have a Hope

And now, dear brothers and sisters,
we want you to know what will happen to the believers who
have died so you will not grieve like people who have no hope.
For since we believe that Jesus died and was raised to life
again, we also believe that when Jesus returns, God will
bring back with Him the believers who have died.

We tell you this directly from the Lord:
We who are still living when the Lord returns
will not meet Him ahead of those who have died.
For the Lord himself will come down from heaven with a
commanding shout, with the voice of the archangel, first
and with the trumpet call of God.
The believers who have died will rise from their graves.
Then, together with them,
we, who are still alive and remain on the earth,
will be caught up in the clouds to meet the Lord in the air.
Then we will be with the Lord forever.
So encourage each other with these words.
1 Thessalonians 4:13-18

I don't know about you, but I love this particular passage of scripture. We all have had those we love transition from this world to the next. Each of us has asked questions about what will happen to their bodies.

Paul tells us in the above passage, when the trumpet sounds, the dead in Christ will rise first. However, Paul really doesn't go into detail. I wanted to know more and so I went to visit I Corinthians 1, and I ended up living there for a few days. The people back in Paul's day were curious, too. That makes me feel better. I'm not the only one who wonders.

161

Paul tells us it's like planting a seed in the ground. The seed is buried in the ground, and after a while, a beautiful flower appears. Ok, so I like that picture.

Let me put it in a way we all will understand. My precious son, Jason, was born with only four fingers on each hand. He had aches and pains his whole life from some very interesting bone structure. Later in life he was diagnosed with an incurable, inoperable cancer. His body was riddled with cancer, and when he died, his body was buried in the ground.

His body was earthly, weak, and corruptible. His body in mortal composition couldn't live forever. Oh, but when the trumpet of the Lord sounds, Jason's body will come up out of the ground and be changed in a moment, in the twinkling of an eye. And that glorified body will rise to meet Jason's spirit which has been with Jesus since he took his final breath of earth's polluted air. Jason's new body will never get sick, it will be perfect, he will have ten fingers, his bone structure will be perfect. He will live forever. Do you understand the precious hope that this mother's heart?

No one who calls themselves by the name of Christ, should be able to think about the resurrection without getting excited. This life isn't all there is. When we walk away from the cemetery after the death of a loved one, when we have followed them as far as we can follow, that's not the end. It's just intermission. Hallelujah!

Prayer

Father, Thank You, this life is not all there is. Thank You that we have a hope. Even in the missing of our loved ones, help us to be reminded of that wonderful hope!

In Jesus' powerful name, Amen!

76
Going God's Way

The Lord Himself goes before you and will be with you;
He will never leave you nor forsake you.
Do not be afraid; do not be discouraged.

Deuteronomy 31:8

God had certainly gone to extraordinary lengths to rescue the Israelites from their long and cruel internment in the prison camp of the Egyptians. In fact, the Bible tells us it was four hundred-thirty years to the day. Don't tell me God isn't interested in details. I think this proves it. He had that rescue planned right down to the minute. He's an on-time God; we can be sure of that.

God, in His divine wisdom didn't take them on the shortest route. He took them the long way around. Don't you know those Israelites complained loud and long? We are like that, aren't we? Sometimes God takes a long time to get us to where we need to be. We struggle, we complain, we scheme, we plan, we try to make things work out, because we think taking the long way around is a waste of time. But I can assure you, when we are traveling with God, taking the long way may not be the easiest way, but it's the right way. In fact, it's the only way, and oh my, the lessons we will learn! Our relationship with the Father will grow deeper, and when we get to where God has been leading us, we will find it has all been worth it. I'd rather take the long arduous journey with God, than to take the short trip on my own.

The Bible tells us they were organized and ready for war when they left Egypt. Once again, God had prepared them for the journey. They knew they would face enemy armies and they were prepared. God didn't leave anything out (did He?) when He sent those people on this journey of a lifetime? He

163

already knew what they would face. And He knows today what we will face, and He is preparing us day by day for what is ahead!

He didn't send them out with no direction. He didn't just say, "Go and figure it out for yourself." He provided heavenly GPS in the form of pillar of cloud and a pillar of fire. He knows the way.

I'll go you one better- He is the way. All we have to do is follow. Sometimes though, we aren't content to just follow. We want to be up front and leading the way. That's pride, my friends. That's thinking we know better than God, and I can guarantee you, it will lead to trouble. Been there! Done that!

So, the Israelites find themselves camped by the Red Sea and they are getting settled in. The women are preparing a meal, the children are playing in the sand, and the men are doing whatever it is the men did. We don't know, but we do know they look up and see Pharaoh's army hot on their trail. They are scared out of their wits, and they turned that fear on Moses.... "Did you just get us out of Egypt so we could die in the wilderness? It would have been better to still be slaves than to die out here." Seriously, I think death would have been an improvement on slavery to Pharaoh, but what do I know?

Moses tells the people, "Just calm down, God's got this. You don't have to do anything. God will fight for you." I love this part of the story. The angel of the Lord that had been leading them, went from in front of them to behind them, and the Pillar of Cloud moved behind them as well.

He takes care of His own. We need to feed at the banquet table of His faithfulness just in this instance. Goodness, if we tried to feed on all the times He's been faithful, we would burst with it all, wouldn't we? I mean we would just blow up.

Well, we know the rest of the story. The Bible tells us God looked at the Egyptians through the pillar of fire, and He troubled them. That's such a poetic way to say his anger was aroused against them.

There is a scripture in Zechariah 2:13 that says," Be silent before the LORD, all humanity, for He is springing into action from his holy dwelling." So, God rolled up His sleeves, and He said, "Look out, I'm going down there!" Scripture tells us He took off their chariot wheels. Of course, by this time they were in the middle of the sea. When God told Moses to stretch out his arm, the waters came down and covered up those Egyptians. Not one of them escaped. I'll tell you what, as those guys were going down for the third time, they knew God was on the throne.

God will go extraordinary lengths to accomplish His will in the lives of people who will only trust and follow. He wants to guide, provide, and protect us. He wants to empower, overshadow, and anoint us. He has a plan for you personally. He knows exactly what you need; and at the appointed time, He will let you in on it.

Prayer

Father, Help me to stop being in such a hurry. Help me to follow you with rejoicing and submit to your timing and your road map.

In Jesus' Name,
Amen!

Notes

77
Spend Time with Jesus

Before daybreak the next morning,
Jesus got up and went out to an isolated place to pray.
Mark 1:35

I'm singing this morning.... "There's nothing worth more that could ever come close, nothing can compare, You're our Living Hope, Your presence Lord!" (Wilson &Torwalt)

I had such a precious time with the Lord this morning. I love being able to lay the needs of others before the throne. I love interceding on behalf of those I love. But most of all, I love basking in the presence of the Father, MY Father. There is something so special about being quiet in the presence of God Almighty. There is peace, joy and contentment as we bask in His love and He delights in ours. Every Christian should have a devotional life, a time spent reading and studying the Word and time spent talking to and listening to the voice of God.

If you find you are struggling in your spiritual walk, if you are weak and more often than not, yielding to temptation, I would ask you, how much time are you spending on your knees? Are you reading the WORD with deliberation, or do you read a short devotion every day before you get out of bed and call that your quiet time? As a Child of God, nothing should come before time dedicated to your relationship with your Heavenly Father, NO THING!!!!!!

I know it's an old song, but it packs a wallop: "Just a Little Talk with Jesus Makes it Right." I can be down and depressed and negative, but when I call on Jesus, He is right there. He changes my attitude and He changes my outlook. The times spent in His presence are relationship building and

Isn't that what it's all about, developing a close personal relationship with God? There's nothing more important than that!

Prayer

Jesus,

If You needed quiet time with the Father, then how much more do I? Please forgive me for not taking time to spend in Your sweet presence. Help me to carve out a time each day to be with You.

In Your most Holy Name,

Amen!

78
Love!

A new commandment I give to you,
that you love one another; as I have loved you...
By this all will know that you are My disciples,
if you have love for one another."
John 13:34-35

Jesus said what He meant and meant what He said. And in this verse, He says it twice just in case we didn't get it the first time.

You know it's interesting to me that He didn't say, "Love the saved only." Or "love the attractive, well dressed, popular, rich and famous." He said, "love one another." Period! The End!

Jesus knew that love conquers all. He knew if we intentionally pursue love that most of our problems will be solved. The devil knows it, too. That's why he worries us so much with reasons not to love. He says things like, "now you know God doesn't expect you to love that person who hurt you." And we jump right on that band wagon, because it's easier not to love than it is to love, especially when we have been hurt. Am I right? You know I am!

We read that scripture like this. A new commandment I give you that you love one another except when .... You fill in the blanks. Now Jesus knew it would be hard for us to love some folks. (Guess what! It's hard for some folks to love us.) But He also knew as we purposefully pursue love, it would bring us rewards both in this world and the next. I can tell you from experience, there is nothing like being able to love your enemy.

169

There is no victory that compares to being able to sincerely pray for the welfare of someone who has egregiously injured you.

You see Jesus knew, even though it wouldn't be easy, it would be invaluable to us in our Christian walk if we went after loving others with everything in us. Love is a risk, but oh so worth it!

Prayer

Lord,

Help me to love like You do without judgment, without partiality.

In Jesus' Name,

Amen

79
Brand New

Therefore, if anyone is in Christ,
he is a new creation;
the old has gone, the new has come!
2 Corinthians 5:17

I love to snuggle in a blanket, with the heat blasting, and listen to Christmas Carols even when Christmas is long gone. Add to that heavy snow falling quietly outside my window and it is perfection.

Outside, the snow, however beautiful, is wet and cold, but we only see the beauty unfolding before us. The dead grass is soon covered with a blanket of white as we watch with the wonder of a child.

And so once were we, just like dead grass. Lifeless, joyless until Jesus came and changed it all. He washed us white as snow. He not only changed our hearts, but He also changed our very lives. He opened our eyes to see the beauty around us He opened our ears to the voice of His Spirit. The grass was greener, and the sky a more vibrant shade of blue.

There really is nothing like snuggling in the arms of Jesus, hearing Him whisper peace to our hearts and minds, while all around us a heavy storm is raging. The thunder crashes, the lightning flashes, outside the wind is howling, but inside we're safe and warm.

And it all started with a visit from an Angel with an announcement: "You shall bring forth a Son and His name will be Jesus."

Let the storms rage, we can nestle in the arms of the Baby who became our Savior.

Prayer

Father,

Thank you for making me brand new. Thank You for the new life I have in You and for the privilege of being Your child and held by You. Thank You that I can rest in peace and safety in Your loving arms.

In Jesus' Name,

Amen!

80
Attitude!

You make known to me the path of life;
in Your presence
there is fullness of joy;
at Your right hand are pleasures forevermore.
Psalm 16:11

It's a glorious day! After weeks of gray, gloomy, wet, muddy, nasty, (you get the picture) weather, the sun is shining. I'm sitting in my office listening to The Percy Faith Orchestra play "A Summer Place." (Don't judge me!) I'm there in that imaginary place. I'm sitting in a beautiful garden with the fragrance of flowers and freshly mown grass. I'm basking in the sunshine and enjoying a humidity-free breeze gently blowing my hair. Wait! I know it's 30 degrees outside, but THE SUN IS SHINING. Isn't it amazing how the sun can change your whole attitude?

Attitude is everything. If we wake up grumpy and take a dim view of the day, then it's likely to be a day full of negatives. But if we face the day with confidence and assurance that whether the sun shines or not, we are going to love, laugh and linger over sweet interchanges with our co-workers, friends and family then chances are, we are going to have a great day! We can make the decision to praise instead of pout, to worship instead of worry, to bless instead of berating! Yes, our attitude changes everything.

Spending time with Jesus is just what we need when we feel ourselves becoming Negative Nellies. It is impossible to spend one moment in His sweet presence without experiencing a turnaround in our way of thinking. He can make what is wrong right, He can turn mishaps into miracles, can change minds and hearts. He can turn the blues into blessings.

He brings grace when we are gloomy. He brings mercy when we are melancholy. I think you get the picture.

Whether it's the weather that's getting you down or something else you can't control that is controlling you, Jesus will help you to let go of it. Yes, He will. He knows how hard it is.

Do you feel like you are living among stinky, stale ashes in a world that looks and feels gray? Jesus wants to bring beauty to your life. Today! Right now!

Prayer

Father,

Help me to have the mind of Jesus, which will give me a glorious attitude. Help me see the beauty around me and to stop to enjoy it and give thanks.

In Jesus' Name, Amen!

81
Jesus Equals Joy

I came that they may have life,
and have it abundantly.
John 10:10

On this dreary January day, the sun is trying so hard to shine, but the gray clouds are keeping it at bay. Our lives our like that sometimes, aren't they? We want to experience joy, but the circumstances of life hold us captive in a gray place where gladness is a stranger. The truth is, life is hard and try as we might, there will always be things that bring us down and attempt to hold us there.

Jesus wants us to live abundantly. And, I can tell you from experience, joy isn't determined by circumstances. It can't be smothered by sorrow, or sickness, loss, or hurt. Joy comes from Jesus. When He sets up housekeeping in our hearts, joy moves right in with Him.

I experienced joy as I stood at the grave of my sweet son. I wasn't happy, my heart was broken, but deep in my heart there was a joy so deep, so wide, so full because I knew my son wasn't in a casket about to be lowered into the cold damp earth. I knew this was not the end, Jason had just walked into Heaven a little sooner than the rest of us, and he would be waiting for us when it was our time.

The joy I experienced that day has continued to bring hope and assurance as the days, months, and years pass by. Jesus wants you to have joy today. He wants to bring beauty from the pile of ashes you call life. You weren't meant to dwell in the ashes, you were created to delight in the Lord blessings! He brings grace experience joy unspeakable and full of glory even if....

Prayer

Father,

    Thank you for the deep down, nothing -can -touch joy that fills my heart. Knowing Jesus, brings joy even when happiness is elusive.

In Jesus' Name, Amen!

Notes

82
We Have Jesus

Weeping may last through the night,
but joy comes with the morning.
Psalm 30:5

It's two days until Thanksgiving. While I'm thankful for all that I have, my heart is heavy for those who have loved ones who are sick and suffering. It's hard to understand.

I recently spoke with a friend whose wife is gravely ill. He shared how he reads in the Word that Jesus is still the same yesterday, today and forever. He said, "Back in those days, Jesus healed everyone who came to Him, so why......?" I told Him I understood his frustration because I've been there and even though we don't understand God, we must trust Him.

Easier said than done. I can tell you; it is so hard to trust when you know God COULD, but He DOESN'T. And how are we supposed to be thankful this year when someone we love is fighting for their very lives?

We can be thankful that a Loving Heavenly Father is faithful, and we are never alone as we walk through this long dark valley. He will provide exactly what we need when we need it. His all-sufficient grace will bring us comfort and peace.

We can be thankful we can approach the throne of God and fall on our faces before Him; and when we can't find the words, the Holy Spirit will pray in the will of God for us.

We were never promised a life without grief, sorrow, and loss, but we were promised we would never live out those difficult times alone. Be thankful each day for the grace and strength provided. Be thankful for a Father Who loves You and Who understands completely what you are going through.

The truth is, everyone goes through difficult, life altering times, but if we have Jesus, we have everything we need to survive whatever it is we are facing. Today and everyday be held in His strong arms. Hold on, child of God! Weeping may endure for the night, but joy comes in the morning!!!

Prayer

Father,

Thank you for your constant presence in my life and for the grace, mercy and love you extend to me.

In Jesus' Name!

Amen!

83
Do What You Can Do

I can do all things through Christ
who gives me strength.
Philippians 4:13

I woke up and went straight to my prayer "closet." I had something I had to do and I dreaded it. Not because it was life threatening but because it was one of those things that was time-consuming and, let me be perfectly honest, boring. It was also important and necessary.

I prayed for the anointing and power of God to fall on me and for the spirit of God to give me a fresh anointing as I began the day. I posted on my Facebook page "I am experiencing the favor of God today."

My first stop on my "adventure" far exceeded my expectations as far as fluidity and ease. The rest of the day didn't go as smoothly as I would have hoped. It was fraught with one roadblock after another. I felt my stress level building. I prayed and plowed on, trusting God all the way to bring the day to a successful end. And you know what? He did! After nearly eight hours of work, work and more work, VICTORY!

The moral of this story is: Just because we have the favor of God on us doesn't mean we can just sit back do nothing. While many times, we are required to sit still and watch God move, there are those times when we have to do what is in our power to do and then God will do what we CAN'T do! And through it all, He is cheering us on and loving us through!

He is magnificent, majestic, and marvelous. At the end of the day, I was exhausted mentally, but spiritually I gained some muscle as I steadfastly marched against the obstacles Satan placed in my way and WON!

Prayer

Father,

Give me the strength to do what I am able to do and the humility to step back and let You do what only You can do.

In Jesus' Name,

Amen!

84
An Appointed Time

I just finished reading the book of Daniel. Several times these words jumped from the pages "at the appointed time." Every time I read those words my heart thrilled with the knowledge that God has a plan. He has an appointed time to answer our prayers. He has an appointed time for miracles. He has an appointed time for all the good things He has planned for us. How absolutely electrifying to know God cares enough about us to plan special times for the things He wants to do for us.

When I was a little girl, I couldn't wait for Christmas (I haven't changed much in that respect). I remember one Christmas Eve I couldn't go to sleep. Daddy said, "Christmas comes at 12:00 am and if you are still awake, you can open your presents."

Guess what! I was wide awake and so we celebrated Christmas very early in the morning that year. My parents gave in to a five-year-old so they could get some rest. But God, well, He doesn't jump the gun. When He appoints a time, IT STAYS APPOINTED. I love the scripture found in Habakkuk 2:3

For the vision is yet for an appointed time.
But at the end it will speak, and it will not lie.
Though it tarries, wait for it.
Because it will surely come, It will not tarry.

There have been times in my life when I have tried to help God out. He wasn't working fast enough to suit me and so I stepped in to give Him a hand. Well, it turns out, He didn't need my help, but I needed His to get out of the mess I created because I thought I was smarter than my Heavenly Father. I forgot to remember God was working while I was waiting. The

181

The Prophet Isaiah writes,

And therefore, will the LORD wait,
that He may be gracious unto you,
and therefore will He be exalted,
that He may have mercy upon you:
for the LORD is a God of judgment:
blessed are all they that wait for Him.
Isaiah 30:18

Recently, I spoke with a friend who had been searching for a job for several months. All through the waiting, I never saw her get discouraged or in a hurry. Every time she went for an interview (there were many) she prayed, "Lord, I want this job only if it's your will and if I don't get it, I won't worry because I know you have a plan." She waited long and she prayed hard, and God gave her exactly the job she wanted and needed. Her faith and steadfastness through the waiting have been an inspiration to me. She waited and the Lord was gracious. God doesn't play favorites; He loves us all the same and He wants to do great things. He is planning great things, and He will be gracious to us if we only wait.

Prayer

Father,

Help me to patiently wait.

Help me not to pace to and fro as I worry about what and when the waiting will end.

I know you will come at the exact moment with the exact answer I need.

In Jesus' Name,

Amen!

85
Stormy Weather

Do any of the worthless idols of the Nations bring rain?
Do the skies themselves send down showers?
No, it is you, LORD our God. Therefore our hope is in You,
for You are the one who does all this.
Jeremiah 14:22

Another, gray, raining, miserable West Virginia Monday. It has been cold and gray and gloomy the entire winter. And now spring has sprung and it's still cold, it's still gray, it's still gloomy!

I happened to mention it to a little old lady I met in Burger King. She said, "You know I don't even notice the gloom." I felt ashamed because there she sat, not able to even walk without the aid of her husband who was nearly as decrepit as she was. So, I thought I'd better put on some Jesus and I said, "It really doesn't matter what the weather is like, if we have Jesus in our hearts." She wholeheartedly agreed.

Reminds me of a song, "It Won't Rain Always." The song speaks of a time when our lives were filled with rain, despair, hurt, and tears. The chorus says:

And it won't rain always.

God's promises are true.

The sun's gonna shine in His own good time.

And He will see you through.

(Wilburn, Gaither)

The fact is, the sun will shine again, and the weather will get warm, and I'll soon be complaining that it's too hot and I'll be longing for those crisp cool fall days. So, until the sun shines again, let's bask in the Son shine, knowing our trials are temporary and God will come at His appointed time and sweep the clouds away.

Prayer

Father,

I love the change of seasons. And I love that in my life I'm not always stuck in the rainy one.

I'm thankful for the season of sunshine and blue skies. I'm thankful You know that I need some of both to grow.

I love you.

In Jesus' Name, Amen!

86
My Shepherd

The Lord is my Shepherd, I shall not want.
Psalm 23:1

So many of us, even though we picture God as a loving Father, we imagine Him sitting on His throne and directing "traffic," pulling strings, and moving mountains from way up somewhere beyond the clouds. We believe He is involved in our lives, but from a distance. Let me correct that error in thinking right this very minute. God is right here with us, right smack dab in the middle of our circumstances. The Bible tells us in Isaiah 41:13 - *For I hold you by your right hand--I, the LORD your God. And I say to you, 'Don't be afraid. I am here to help you.*

Does that sound to you like He is far away? I don't think so. I'm teaching from a book written by W. Phillip Keller, A Shepherd Looks at the Twenty-third Psalm. He tells how the flock can be agitated and frightened easily, but when the Shepherd walks into their midst, they become calm. Why? Because as dumb as they are, they know this: The Shepherd cares about them, He will protect them. He will feed them. Whatever they need, their Shepherd will provide. They know this because He is a faithful shepherd. They have learned through experience that He will meet their every need.

Sound familiar? No wonder the Bible calls us sheep. It is so wonderful to hear the Shepherd's voice in times of difficulty! It is refreshing to be able to lie down in green pastures beside Him and just "be." It's so invigorating to walk with Him in paths of righteousness and to experience emotional and spiritual healing as He leads beside still waters.

Today in whatever circumstance you find yourself, Your Shepherd is there right beside you, holding your hand. He will do whatever is necessary to give you what you need. Be encouraged! Take heart! Be at peace! He has it all under control!

PRAYER

Father,
Help me to follow you as sheep follow their Shepherd. Help me to remember You are all I need. In Jesus' Name, Amen

87
Life's Mysteries

All Scripture is inspired by God and profitable for teaching,
for reproof, for correction, for training in righteousness.
2 Timothy 3:16

There are so many mysteries in this life, so many questions! Answers that are illusive. Life itself is a mystery.

I don't know about you, but I'm constantly and intentionally searching for answers. And I think we must face the fact that we may not get every answer we are looking for. I had one mystery solved for me today. It's something I've been thinking about, well, since I was a teenager. I consulted people in whom I had great confidence. I conferred with friends. I read books. I watched talk shows and never got a solution that satisfied me. Have you ever been in such a place?

While the mystery wasn't exactly a huge issue, as winter melted into spring, and summer gave way to the beauty of autumn, I continued to be perplexed. I agonized that I would do the wrong thing at the wrong time and if I did commit such a faux pas, would I then be the object of ridicule?

I am usually confident, but in this situation, I was reduced to mousey, miserable insecurity. To even think about it brought me angst. Could no one give me an answer that even made sense to me?

Well, I got an answer that made my day, my week, my year. Out of the blue, I was watching Brandy, White House Black Market Fashion BFF, and the whole segment was the answer to my question. YES, YOU CAN WEAR WHITE BEFORE MAY 30 AND ALSO AFTER LABOR DAY. Do you know how freeing that is for someone like me? Well, I can tell you, I am free at last!

Now I'm going to give you the reason wearing white was restricted to those days Between Memorial Day and Labor Day. It seems the wealthy ladies in the big cities retired to their summer homes at the lake, the beach, or wherever their summer homes happened to be. They left the city the day after Memorial Day and returned the day after Labor Day. When they returned to the city, no wearing of whites occurred. Since the society ladies weren't wearing white, the rest of the town didn't either. And y'all, we've been in bondage to that idea ever since. Oh, the wasted springs, falls, and winters that our whites lay dormant when we could have been enjoying them year-round. Very interesting to see how tradition can take over, and even more noteworthy, that we all buy into what someone says is right or wrong.

We can be that way in our spiritual lives, too, can't we? We can read a book or hear a minister speak and right away we assume what we have read or heard is truth? Am I right? You know I am.

I encourage you, don't believe what books or preachers tell you, if they aren't backed by the truth of the Word of God. Don't just read the Bible; study it. Who is writing? To whom are they writing? What was the culture of the time of the writing? What do the key words mean in Hebrew (Old Testament) or Greek (New Testament). You know you can google Greek and Hebrew meanings, right? You can also google many different commentaries that will explain so many things. Well, if you didn't, now you do.

I was talking to someone one day and they spouted off a litany of their beliefs regarding a certain subject. My answer was, "Oh, where in scripture did you find that?" (Knowing full well, it wasn't in Word.) The reply was, "Oh, I don't know the scripture, but I heard a preacher say it!"

Voilà! That's how people are misled. READ the Word, STUDY the Word and you will KNOW the truth and the truth will set you free. As you read and study, the Holy Spirit will confirm in your heart the truth you seek.

While I'm so excited I can wear white all four seasons now, I will not trust the answers to my questions of eternal importance to a talk show host, a book I read, or a preacher. I will ask the Holy Spirit to open my eyes of understanding as I read and study the Word that was God breathed into the hearts and minds of men who were available, who had ears to hear and hearts to obey.

Prayer

Father,

Your Word is the final word. Help me to trust your Word and your heart. You will never lead me astray. Help me to stay in your Word and may it find fertile soil in my heart.

In Jesus' Name, Amen!

Notes

88
A New Year

Let all that I am wait quietly before God,
for my hope is in him.
He alone is my rock and my salvation,
my fortress where I will not be shaken.
My victory and honor come from God alone.
He is my refuge, a rock where no enemy can reach me.
O my people, trust in him at all times.
Pour out your heart to him, for God is our refuge.

Psalm 61:1-2,6-8

This year, I did not start the year with resolutions. I began with counting my blessings. The weeks leading up to Christmas were fraught with many unexpected events. I am so enthralled by the mercy and grace of God in getting us through those terrifying, trying times. It began one night with a Ladies Tea my cousins (three of them) had attended. They had a wonderful time. They sent pictures of the three of them together and I was jealous because distance prevented me from joining them.

As they left to go to their respective homes, one of them made a wrong turn and found herself on a very narrow road. The right tire of her car went off the road and landed on an unstable shoulder. The car tipped and rolled over a twenty-foot embankment and landed on its roof.

My cousin, like the rest of our family, is made of strong stuff. She managed to release the seat belt and was able to move about the car, trying to locate her phone to call for help. I confess as she shared that experience, we laughed. I had a

191

vision of her crawling around in the upside-down car. At the same time, my mind drifted to the "what if she had managed to cause the car to begin to roll again."

She was unable to find her phone and she wondered in the dark how long it would take for her to be found. She had no phone; she was over the hill in a remote area, and she resigned herself to spending the night in the car. She is brave, that's for sure. She's brave because she prayed God would send help and she believed He would.

God works in ways we cannot understand. The horn of the car began to sound, beep, beep, beep, moments of silence, then beep, beep, beep. The horn continued that routine until the EMS arrived.

Unknown to my cousin, a ninety-four-year-old lady heard the horn. She called a neighbor who was a firefighter and said, "I think someone has gone over the hill, I can hear a horn, can you check it out?" He did and much to his surprise, he found the car with my cousin in it. She was alert and talking. He called the EMS, and they were able to extricate her without further issues.

Well, the story does not end there. She was taken to a trauma center where she received scans, blood work, x-rays, you name it. They found nothing. No broken bones, no internal injuries, nothing. It was a miracle. Oh, did I mention my cousin is eighty-one? I asked her if she was scratched and bruised. She reported a small bruise on her shoulder. I am shaking my head.

After we heard the news, our family circled the throne in prayer. That is what we do, and God heard us. He is faithful! Now that is the best Christmas present ever.

A few days before that another cousin's son had an accident, his car was totaled. He is fine.

Not many days following, the car my husband was driving was hit and totaled. No injuries.

A week or so later, a battery blew up in another cousin's face. He was injured, but it could have been worse. It missed his eye, no battery acid got on him. He may have a scar, but he is alive and well.

Aren't you glad you are not related to me? It has been a scary couple of weeks. However, through it all, the presence of God has been near. You may ask, "Why would God let all of that happen to one family?" I don't know and what's more, it is none of my business. My business is to pray and trust.

I know sometimes things do not work out as positively as our circumstances have. I've received "no" answers to some serious prayers. I didn't like the answer. I was disappointed in the answer, but I trusted God who does all things well.

And so, on this bright, shiny, clean New Year, I simply want to thank the Lord for His goodness through the good times and the not so good. We can trust Him. And as we walk into the unknown before us, let's look forward with excitement and expectation of the adventures our God will lead us through.

He can be depended on!

Prayer

Father,

Life can be difficult, disappointing, and sometimes devastating. Through it all, there You are, always present, always patient, always providing. I am glad we have You to lean on during those confusing and often frustrating times. You love us with a love we cannot fathom, yet we are thankful. Help us to keep our eyes on you.

In Jesus, sweet Name,
Amen!

Notes

89
Undeserved, but Freely Given

Because of His grace He made us right in His sight
and gave us confidence that
we will inherit eternal life.
Titus 3:7

Sitting in my quiet place with the Lord one day, I immediately was filled with the peace that comes from being connected to the Father. I began, "Lord, what I have done that made me deserving of your presence?" The truth is I have made some huge mistakes and not just once, but more times than I care to remember and yet, God has been so gracious and merciful to me. I shudder when I think where I would be without the grace of my Heavenly Father.

The Holy Spirit brought to mind people I had written off because of some offense aimed at me, or someone I love. I will confess even though I have walked with the Lord most of my life, my first response when affronted, is to get even. It's the human in me. It's my personality. Ah, yes, in the past, I tried to excuse it by saying, "It's just the way I am." And I know Jesus loves me, "just the way I am," but as Max Lucado says, "He loves me too much to leave me that way."

During my journey on this narrow road, Jesus has brought me to some things that have taught me some things. Sometimes I am a slow learner and yet His patience is unwavering. So, I kept taking the test, over and over and over again, until one day, I finally passed. This is not to say I'm not tempted toward vengeance when someone hurts me. What I can tell you is: the Holy Spirit immediately calls to mind the long suffering of my Savior and I instantly lay down my plan to settle the score at the feet of the One who was offended beyond endurance, and yet endured to the end.

Jesus has been there. Peter, who vowed to love Him and never leave Him, denied Him three times. The disciplines conveniently disappeared when He was arrested. The soldiers mocked Him, spit on Him, slapped Him, beat Him, placed a crown of thorns on His head and crucified Him. And yet He loved them to the end.

In life, things don't always go our way. Sometimes, it's because we go our way, and it is the wrong way. Often, circumstances prevent us from getting what we want. Sometimes people may stand in the way. Sometimes we get in our own way. Jesus never promised we would have a perfect, peaceful, pressure free life. But He did promise He would give us what we needed to get through. And it all began with grace. All sufficient, amazing, undeserved grace. Freely given by the only One who had the right to take vengeance on us.

I'm glad he chose grace. I'm glad He offered grace where punishment was deserved. And He offers it minute by minute, day by day.

Now, if we are going to be Christ followers, am I right in deducing that we must offer that same grace? I believe wholeheartedly that we are. You see, in loving others, in allowing love to cover a multitude of wrongs, I am being conformed into the image of Jesus. And isn't that what it's all about?

Prayer

Father,

Thank you for the amazing grace I experience daily.
Help me to extend your grace
to those who have offended me.
In Jesus' Name,
Amen!

90
God Sings!

For the LORD your God is living among you.
He is a mighty savior.
He will take delight in you with gladness.
With his love, He will calm all your fears.
He will rejoice over you with joyful songs.
Zephaniah 3:17

What? God sings over us? What a profound thought and I loved it so much. I read it again and something caught fire in my spirit. God sings over me! I bring Him joy! What a thought! Insignificant though I may be, I bring joy to the Father. And, beloved, so do you!

I try to imagine what kind of voice God has, and someone asked, "Do you suppose He makes up songs about us? And what would they be?" Later on my husband and I were talking about it and he said, "I wonder if He sings all four parts at the same time?"

Of course we don't know the answer to any of these questions. But I do know this: to hear my Father sing with joy over me would be the most beautiful sound I ever heard. He delights in us. He rejoices over us. We bring Him great joy! The wonder of it all takes my breath away! I love being His child.

Prayer
Father, What a wonderful truth to know I bring joy to Your heart. May my words, my thoughts, the encounters I have with others continue to bring delight to you as I walk in obedience.
In Jesus' Name, Amen!

He will give a crown
of beauty for ashes,
a joyous blessing
instead of mourning,
festive praise instead of despair.

Isaiah 61:1-3

Made in the USA
Monee, IL
22 May 2023

34353371R00118